WEEP NO MORE, MY PEOPLE

By

Kaz Kucharek

ISBN 0-88925-616-0

Published by
Byzantine Books
1747 Toronto St.
Regina, Saskatchewan S4P 1M5
Canada

First printing, 1985

Printed and bound in Canada by
Friesen Printers
a Division of D. W. Friesen & Sons Ltd.
Altona, Manitoba R0G 0B0
Canada

By the same author:

The Rite of Holy Matrimony (Ukrainian News, Edmonton, Alberta, 1962)

The Divine Liturgy (in collaboration with Rev. A. Muzyka: Re-
 deemer's Voice Press, Yorkton, Saskatchewan, 1968)

The Byzantine-Slav Liturgy of St. John Chrysostom (Alleluia
 Press, 1971)

To Settle Your Conscience (Our Sunday Visitor, 1974)

The Sacramental Mysteries, A Byzantine Approach, (Alleluia
 Press, 1976)

Our Faith, A Byzantine Catechism for Adults, (Alleluia Press, 1983)

Dedicated

To the people I adopted as my own,
We prayed together, worked together,
Sharing each hardship and joy.
At times we laughed.
Sometimes we cried.
Sharing our lives,
Most of all, in love,
They gave me their heart,
Honestly, sincerely.
And I gave them mine.
When I am gone, they will weep.
But I shall wipe their tears
And tell them:
Weep no more, my people,
Weep no more.

Foreword

This book is different. No, it was not written by a disgruntled priest, nor even by one who disagrees with any of the Church's doctrines or discipline. Neither does it contain any romantic interludes or scandalous tidbits to spice up its pages. If that is your cup of tea, then this book is not for you.

Simply put, this work is an account of a pastor's experiences, actual human interest events which will tug at the heart-strings of any reader. In the life of any "man of the cloth" situations arise which are joyous and humorous but others are tragic and soul-wrenching, filled with pathos and poignancy. These provide revealing glimpses into the heart and feelings of any pastor who loves his people and what happens to him outside the church services and his regular round of duties.

Of course, the people understand that a priest or minister is a person like anyone else. He once wore diapers and learned to speak like everyone else. He was heckled by schoolmates, was punished by his parents and suffered the uncertainties and confusion of adolescence — everything any young person goes through. As a grown-up, as a pastor, he is not much different — there he is speeding, sweating, frowning, teaching, fishing and, yes, golfing, and in general trying to live up to half of what he preaches. These things people know.

What many do not realize are the things that happen to a man of the cloth about which they know very little: his feelings, emotions, his recreation and, above all, his counsel which changes or affects persons for life — and for eternity. Some of the instances described in this book may help people understand, in whatever little way, their own pastor, his strains and stresses which he has to undergo many times.

So when you catch him at a bad moment try to be a bit more patient and understanding why he does not seem to care whether the Ladies' Auxiliary wish to buy eight Easter lilies instead of six and just where they should be placed. He may have just come from a dying person and a home where the family has never experienced the death of a loved one. The number of Easter lilies and where to put them is indeed trivial in comparison, but that does not mean that "he doesn't care about his parish."

Though the events described in this book are true, all names of people resembling the living or the dead are entirely fictional.

I wish to express my gratitude to my volunteer secretary, Mrs. Rose Strahm, for typing the manuscript of this book. I honor it with the title manuscript but most of its pages looked more like Egyptian or cuneiform hieroglyphs than a readable copy of English. With all the correctives, crossed out words and sentences, arrows indicating new ones inserted above or below the lines or in the margins, new paragraphs and what not, I am sure Mrs. Strahm spent more time and energy attempting to decipher the manuscript rather than in the actual typing of the work.

I thank her also for looking after the rectory-office work, attending the door-bells and telephones so that I would be able to devote more time for writing this book.

My thanks also to Karl, her husband, for allowing her time to work for me and especially for being patient enough to listen to every episode described in the book without derogatory comments.

K.K.

Table of Contents

Wet Behind the Ears but Gung-Ho

Freshly ordained! First assignment: second assistant at St. George's Cathedral Parish. Though that meant the lowest rank on the totem pole, second doormat, if you will, I was still very gung-ho, a budding starry-eyed zealot waiting for a crusade to happen. Certainly I was going to do all sorts of good things for Saskatoon, nay, for the whole wide world.

Maybe that was why my boss, the pastor, ever so knowingly but no less indulgently kept smiling at my attitude. You know that type of smile that the cat has after he eats the canary and his owner sagely smiles back which silently tells him, "Boy, are you going to get it now!"

Well, I put it down to the pastor's old age, a man who had probably lost his vim and vigor somewhere along the line. Who knows, maybe he never had it in the first place.

That "Boy, *are you going to get it now*" started the next day from all sides. No big deal, just little things at first. They had no housekeeper-cook at the rectory. It was strictly every man for himself. So the next day after the Eucharistic Liturgy, I rushed down the block to the confectionery for some bacon and eggs and back to the rectory.

Always in a rush, I figured why do something in ten minutes when one can do it in three. So I put the burner on high, cracked the eggs straight into the pan, then the bacon. Ah, it smelled good, just like the breakfasts mother used to make. I luxuriated in that aroma for a few blissful minutes. One minute too long, I am afraid. All of a sudden, the thin slices of

1

bacon just disappear in a puff of smoke. Cannot believe my eyes! I may not be a chef at Maxime's — to be honest, I did not even make the grade as short-order cook at Greasy's Diner back home, but I do have wonderful powers of deduction. "Bet I had the heat on too high," I whisper to myself (even at that tender age I talked to myself).

Oh well, I still have the eggs but I better put them aside or they too might go puff and disappear in a cloud of smoke.

Now for the toast. Oh sure, forgot to buy some bread. Rush back to the confectionery, put two slices of rye into the toaster and light up a cigarette. As I'm sitting, I wipe my brow and wonder why they did not teach us a little bit of home economics in the seminary instead of six years of Latin, five of Greek and all those other very useful subjects like Cicero, Virgil or Homer without which a person cannot get along for even a day!

What? Smoke again! O yo-yo-joj, the toast is burning! I retrieve the toast but it is inedible. Well, I still have the eggs!

Ya, the eggs. They are cold, seared at the bottom and raw, very raw at the top. I spit out the first bite. Somewhat despondent at my first failure, I put on the suit coat and head for the nearest restaurant.

The next day, fully determined that no mere bacon and eggs defeat me, I tackle the job again. I do not forget the milk either. I am not an idiot, you know; I did get a 95% average in Latin and Greek. So there!

Out come the frying pan, the bacon and eggs. I put the heat on low to medium (to be honest, I asked the pastor about that one and he said the bacon should also be cooked first). The bacon came out perfectly. See, I'm learning. Now for the eggs. I crack one into the pan. Perfect, I didn't even break the yolk. Now for the other one. Crack. When the smell of its green insides hit me, I gasp and, like the radio announcer at the disaster of the dirigible Hindenburg at Lakehurst, New Jersey, utter in disbelief, "My God." Unlike him, however, I run across the house to the bathroom to retch and reel.

The smell reaches the bathroom and, if anything, becomes stronger by the second. Oh, no, in my haste I forgot to take the frying pan off the burner! With handkerchief over my nose and mouth I race back to the kitchen, grab the frying pan and run outside and dump the whole thing into the garden, pan and all. Now be brave, Kucharek, you have to go right back in there and open all the windows.

That done, again I reach for my suit coat and head for the nearest restaurant!

Now after twenty-nine years, I still do not shine in the culinary department. My version of a meal fit for kings is a can of soup, peas or corn from my favorite supermarket, carefully warmed up, and cold-cuts. No, Virginia, fried eggs do not come in cans! Better boil the eggs for breakfast at least, I found that they do not burn.

Doing the laundry was easy, I thought, at least you cannot burn the clothes in the washer. Come Monday morning I get together a bundle of my personal clothes and bed linens, put them in the middle of my room, and rush off to celebrate the Liturgy.

After breakfast (in a restaurant, of course . . . where else do gourmets eat?), I go to my room for the bundle. There on top of it is the pastor's huge mother cat with her brood of six kittens, snug as the proverbial bugs in the rug. Showing utmost consideration (which every wise assistant does to his boss's cat), I gently shoo them off the pile and bend over to pick up the clothes. **Phew!** The mother cat did not do it, I know, for

3

she had been housebroken ages ago. The cute, fluffy kittens look up at me innocently as if to say, "Who? Us?"

Rather gingerly I dump the clothes into the washer and put in the detergent. Then on with the washer cover and turn on the cycle. Simple, really.

As the machine purrs on like the pastor's cat, I sit down to read Thomas Acquinas's *Summa Theologica;* what else would a bright young assistant enjoy reading but pious, learned volumes like that? Agatha Christie, that's what!

The washer does not flood, does not blow up; nor is there any earthquake, tornado, or fire and the cycle is done. Knowing my luck with things mechanical, I figure, no possibility can entirely be excluded.

No fires, no floods, but the clothes somehow do not turn out exactly as the ad on the box claimed: **For sparkling whites. With color-safe and fabric-safe bleach.** Well, my fabrics are indeed safe, my colored clothes are safe too. I know, I examine each article as carefully as does a mother the fingers and toes on her newly-born babe. My whites are sparkling all right but sparkling with every color of the rainbow!

At least if they were sparkling with red, white and blue I could wear the T-shirts and chuck it up to patriotism (at that time Canada used the British flag); maybe I could stretch that to include my white dress shirts too, but red, green, black, orange, navy blue, pink and a kind of ratty grey? For the love of me, I cannot think of any flag in the world that includes *all those colors.* I am not quite sure what colors the flags of Basutoland or Burundi have but surely not all those colors!

What to do? I cannot afford to throw away all those clothes. "Above all, do not panic," the top sarge used to say, "sit down, assess the situation and think things out." The first three are always easy but it is the thinking out that always presented the difficulty. Even Agatha Christie's Miss Marple would not be able to solve this one, I muse. Wait a minute — I told you I was smart — I have a turtle-neck sweater and I can wear that over any of those multicolored shirts and nobody will be the wiser. Whether this be an ingenious solution or a dopey idea, I must hang out the clothes to dry (the rectory does not have a dryer).

Putting all the shirts at the bottom of the laundry basket or whatever one calls that basket every knowledgeable housewife has when she hangs out the family wash, I grab the bag of clothespins and charge out to the clothesline. By that time all the neighboring ladies are already gathering up *their dried* wash and smile indulgently at my tardiness, probably thinking I slept in after a hot party with the Youth Club the night before. Good for you, ladies. Being good Catholics they all smile, all except one, our very next door neighbor. She looks my way, purses her lips, jerks up her head and indignantly struts off to her house. She must be Protestant, I speculate (ecumenism had not established even a toe-hold in my thoughts as yet: the poor lady turned out to be head of our altar society)!

Beginning with the socks, working ever so slowly, I save my streaked multi-hues towards the end. There is reason for my scheming: by the time I get to my rainbow hues, all of the ladies hopefully will be gone. They are. Only a few items are left and WHAM a screen-door slams and Mrs. Pursed Lips comes out to reel in her one scarf still on the line. She looks my way, sees my shirts and utter horror hits her face with the force of a left hook to the jaw. Leaving her scarf on the line, she scampers back into her house. By the time I finish, telephones are buzzing throughout the neighborhood. Nice woman, Mrs. Pursed Lips.

When, finally, everything is dry I go to gather in

the wash. I do not break a leg nor even sprain an ankle but right in the middle of each shirt, sock and hanky is a dirty rust line from the cable-type clothesline! Elementary for everyone except me but how was I to know that the line is supposed to be wiped with a cloth before hanging up any wash. Just what else can befall my shirts? Makes a preacher swear though — and a priest too! Believe me, gathering in the sheaves seems easier than doing the laundry or cooking for that matter.

By the way, my turtle-neck got a lot of use that summer. It worked like a charm, except during eighty-five- and ninety-degree weather. With everyone in short sleeves, including ninety-year-olds, I sweltered in my turtle-neck, looking silly and sweat pouring out of every pore. I do not know how the people regarded their odd young assistant but I do know what the pastor was thinking: *ha, the one who was going to conquer Saskatoon, man, are you getting it now and these are just small things. Wait till you get to the spiritual side of the parish.*

And he smiles!

Mother Pin a Medal On Me

The inability to cook a good meal or do the laundry did not make me slash my wrists or jump off a plane somewhere between Saskatoon and Winnipeg. I was still gung-ho all right but no less wet behind the ears as I plunged into the pastoral life of the parish.

A Funny Thing Happened at the Rectory Yesterday. Yes, it did. We had many knights of the road, itinerants, who came to the rectory for handouts. It happened on the day I got my first monthly check: seventy-five dollars.

I answer the doorbell. The man wants five bucks for a night's lodging. Fair enough, five bucks would not get anyone into the Ritz but it would do at one of the down-at-the-heels hotels on Twentieth Street. After cashing the check and buying some much needed groceries, I do not have the proper change. I give the man a twenty and tell him to get me change. I would give him the five spot when he comes back!

I know you are laughing. The pastor happens to overhear it all. He winces and laughs . . . rather indecorously: "Do you for one minute think the man will come back?" Somewhat naively, I reply, "Well, of course he will, he's got my twenty!"

We wait five minutes, the five stretch into ten, then fifteen. There is no sign of the man. This time the pastor tells me straight off the cuff, "Sucker, there is one born every minute."

Then the doorbell again. All out of breath, the man comes in. Clutching the change for the twenty in his fist, he apologizes, "Sorry, Father, but the first store was closed, so I had to go to the next one. Here is your change." I give him the five and he is gone. I look at the pastor: his smile gone now, he exclaims, "Well, I'll be . . . bet that doesn't happen but once in ten thousand."

Wish I could say that the life of a priest in a parish, any parish, is a series of lighthearted incidents reminiscent of *Going My Way* or *Bells of St. Mary's*. Well, it is not. Mostly it is facing heart-wrenching tragedy, suffering and death, always painfully moving, sometimes piercing the core of one's being. It is also grappling with domestic troubles, anxieties, worries of mothers and fathers, of husbands and wives, of the young and the old.

Even today as I look back on twenty-nine years of priestly life and everything comes into focus, the pains of people, their sufferings and sorrows crowd out the happy incidents. In short, the world about us is hurting deeply, drowning in its own tears.

Take my first emergency sick call. A sixty-year-old man drops on the street. Heart attack. The ambulance rushes him to City Hospital and he is D.O.A. (Dead on Arrival). The family is notified. I am notified.

By the time I get there he is on the slab in the hospital morgue. As I give him the Last Rites, Extreme Unction, conditionally (generally, this sacrament can be given up to two hours after apparent death, for no one knows when the soul actually separates from the body), my hands shake so badly I can hardly hold the prayer book. It is difficult enough for a priest to administer any sacrament for the first time but to give the Last Rites when true death may set in any second is something which can be very nerve-shattering indeed.

That done, I go out to the waiting room to see the widow, daughters and son. What can be done to ease their shock, to stem their tears? Maybe there is no real

8

answer. *Dear God, help me to say and do the right things to ease their sorrow,* I pray as I walk down the corridor to the waiting room. Moving up a chair close to the grieving widow, silently, I take her hands into mine.

"Tell me, please tell me, Father, he is not dead, he cannot be. He was never sick in his whole life. How can he be dead? He's not. He's not. Tell me that, Father." With that, she stands up and looks pleadingly into my eyes.

Standing up, I put my arms around her shoulders, my head touching hers, "My dear, I don't know what to say. I know what you are going through. I know. Cry it all out now, don't hold anything back. Death is not the end of everything for him. It is a separation for awhile, it is true, and that's why it's sad. But for him it is the beginning of eternal, never ending life. He'll be waiting for you, my dear."

I stay with her about an hour. By then the shock is not really over, but the crisis of shock is.

The next shock of death comes that same evening. This time at the home of an old Ukrainian couple, married fifty-eight years. When the phone call comes in, I grab the holy oils and rush out — without asking whether the man could still swallow the Communion-bread. Inexperience.

True enough, the man is deathly sick, but still very clear-minded. He confesses with the beautiful simplicity of a child, gratefully receives the Last Anointing, presses my hand and smiles. He tells the family gathered around his bed, "the thread of my life is just about broken but do not grieve for me." No regrets. No fear. Not having brought the sacred host along I tell the family that I will be back in fifteen minutes.

It took a little longer. In the meantime the Doctor was there and had given him a sedative. When I get back, the old man is sleeping but his wife awakens him. The old man shakes his head as if to get the cobwebs out of his mind. He receives Christ in the host very piously. We pray a little. I tiptoe out of the sick room, talk with the family and, as we all look into his room five minutes later, he is dead.

The autoposy shows he died of a ruptured aorta. The autopsy report also stated that about thirty years back his aorta ruptured and had healed itself! Apparently, the blood congealed and formed a protective cover about the size of a goose egg. He should have been dead thirty years before that.

A few days later. Death again. The call comes in about 2:00 o'clock at night. They just brought a man in from Yellow Creek by air-ambulance. I grab the sick-call set and rush out to St. Paul's Hospital two blocks away. As I hurry down the street, black bag in hand, the feeling of being on a movie set steals over me. It is almost unreal. So many deaths in the past week.

Yes, he is dying. His wife who came by air-ambulance with him is in hysterics. The nurses are trying their best to calm her. They do not succeed. She cries and screams, cries and screams. The Last Rites, some prayers, some gurgling in the throat and that is it. *May the Lord have mercy on your soul, Wasyl.*

Together with the nurses we break the news to her as gently as we can. She is beside herself with grief, completely hysterical. I phone for her sons to come and pick her up and tell them about their father. By the time they can get to Saskatoon, it will be about eight in the morning. Someone will have to take her in until then. Cannot call any of the parishioners because of the late hour. Nothing to do but take her to the rectory. Walk back to get the car and ask the pastor's permission to bring her in. He concurs. I bring her in with my car.

Up the rest of the night, trying to calm her down. When her sons come to get her in the morning, she still is out of it. She probably does not know what has happened at all for words simply do not reach her. She is just crying and crying.

Way down deep, something must have registered, however, for that Christmas some months later she sent a cake, *kobasa* (homemade sausage) and cookies, with the note: "Till my dying day I shall never forget your kindness when I needed it the most."

Another day, another week. St. Paul's calling: "Father, can you come to Emergency right away. We have an apparent rape victim here, maybe you can help."

"Sure, I'll be right there."

Get briefed (gaining experience fast) by the resident doctor in charge of the "case" (I hate the word *case;* it is a human being not an impersonal case). She was dumped at Emergency. Her name is Jane.

In the cubicle, Jane is completely out of her mind; she has totally lost control of reality. The nurses are trying desperately to hold her down.

"My God, my God, both of us are going to hell, into everlasting fire, my God, my God," Jane wails.

"Listen, Jane, listen. You are not going to hell. We are all your friends here. We are going to help you. Can you hear me?"

"Aow, aow, I am going to hell-fire — hell fire, hell fire," her voice trails off, only to begin screaming a half minute later.

So it went on for an hour. Nothing could be done, only sedatives — a cop out for some, a saviour for others.

After Jane spent six months in the Saskatchewan University Psychiatric Ward and five more in the North Battleford Mental Institution, she came back home, able to function on her own but she was never the same again.

So it went on week after week, month after month. Death, sorrow, tragedy, and pain. Death, sorrow, tragedy and pain. That is the story of any priest's life, or for that matter, any non-Catholic minister's life. Do not pity us, however.

Believe me, do not pity us. We have chosen this life of service. We live it gladly. But do not hassle us in your meetings about "not taking any interest in the life of the parish," it's many meetings and suppers.

When one is dying, believe me, those fund-raising dinners, teas, dances, or what have you, really are nothing in comparison, especially if not done out of the spirit of love.

Yes, for the year I was there, it was telephone duty, doorbells and meetings. These became routine but tragedy and death never became routine. They never are.

I Will Never Forget You, My Friend

It is true: the door to the human heart can be opened only from the inside. Well, old Jacob Bernstein opened his heart to me and I opened mine to him on many an occasion. Before he went to the God of Abraham, Isaac and Jacob (his namesake), he gave me a lovely *talis,* the Jewish prayer shawl, and he asked me to recite the *kaddish,* the mourner's prayer each year on the anniversary of his death. It is usually recited by the children of the deceased. Our friendship was so close that he regarded me as a son and I, in turn, was proud of this singular honor. I would have been pleased to be his natural son.

We first met in Saskatoon in 1956. He was sitting on a park bench, tears silently trickling from his eyes, down his face until they disappeared into his white beard.

I sat down beside him, hoping my Roman collar lent an air of sincere solicitude, and asked, "Grandpa, may I be of help?

He looked up somewhat startled and sadly smiled, "No, I'll be all right. You see I lost my Sarah two months ago before the grass was green and the daffodils bloomed. We used to come here every summer to enjoy the warmth, the grass and the flowers. I was just thinking of her."

We talked for awhile and, finally, went to the Bessborough for coffee. He invited me to his house and a beautiful friendship began, a friendship that became ever closer in the ensuing years.

In his day, Jacob had made a fortune, lost it, and began anew. He wanted lots of children but it was not to be, not even one to carry on his family's blood lines. He was a good man, though, considerate and kind towards all. Once a young ruffian laughed at him in derision, calling him a dirty Yid: through my anger I only saw a smart-alecky, brutal punk but old Jacob held up his hand — and saw in him a young wounded human being.

Generally, we would talk and talk, over checkers, over cribbage, over coffee or by the fireside. He was a lonely man now and he would tell me about his life, his struggles, temptations and his deep feeling for Sarah, the only love of his life. He and his father had been survivors of New Jerusalem, the first Jewish farming community in Saskatchewan which failed.

One day, after hearing him describe his extraordinary struggles and experiences on the wintry prairie as a ten-year-old on the way to Estevan in search of a fellow villager from the Western Ukraine, I told him, "Jacob, someday I'm going to write and tell the world about it." Brushing his bushy white beard against my face and innocently gazing into my soul, he embraced me and said, "I know you will, Father Kaz, I know you will."

This, then, is his account of what happened. I merely put flesh on his words and made his record more vibrant.

*   *   *

The blizzard raged on.

For Yitsak Bernstein and his ten-year-old son, Jacob, there was no East or West, North or South as they trudged on. The razor-sharp, howling wind cut into every fiber of their bodies, piercing their thick coats, pants and underwear, chilling, numbing the marrow of their bones.

Their eyes, almost swollen shut, burned in their sockets. Hoarfrost clung to Yitsak's beard and eyebrows. From under his cap his long hair hung in strands of congealed ice. Both father and son stooped lower and lower as they squared their shoulders to stumble on hour after hour.

It was getting harder and harder to breathe. Each gasp for air seared their lungs. They had no idea where they were. Lost souls in a swirling sea of white.

They pause.

"Yekele," Yitsak almost always used the affectionate, diminutive form to his son, "we will have to stop here. The blizzard will probably last for another day anyway. This is bald prairie country, so we will have to dig a hole in the snow to get out of the wind. Maybe, with God's help, we will sleep better than last night."

"I hope so, Papa. I hope so . . ." Jacob's voice was almost totally lost in the full fury of the storm.

"This is as good a place as any, Yekele. Too bad there are no trees or rushes around. We could use their branches for bedding."

They clawed at the packed, hardened snow. For every two handfuls thrown out of the deepening hole, one swirled back in. They made slow, painful progress, but progress nevertheless, and after what seemed an eternity to Jacob, the hole was large enough to hold them both.

They laid down side by side in it, ate some frozen bread and settled in for the long night. Yitsak put his arm around Jacob's shoulder as if to shield him from the biting wind which quickly covered their bodies with a thick coating of snow.

"Yekele. . . ."

"Yes, Papa?"

"God is good. There are many things in life that we have to suffer. Sometimes too many. Often we think that we cannot go on. But God always gives us strength. When your mother Hannah died three years ago, I thought it was the end of me. My heart died within me too. Ach, I kept telling myself that I had to live for you but all I could feel was emptiness, a big black void from the rising of the sun to the going down of the same.

"The emptiness, Yekele, is still there but you have filled much of it. You have her eyes, her nose, and her heart. You have been a great consolation to me these last three years.

"Someday, Yekele, you will have somebody to love and cherish as I did Hannah. May she bring you as much happiness as Hannah did to me. But first you must get educated and then work hard, very hard, so that you will have a nest of your own. My greatest desire is to have grandchildren. You must give me many grandchildren so that the name Bernstein will never die out, that it will be multiplied as the sand on the seashore.

"I may never see them or the laughter in their eyes. I haven't been feeling too well lately. No, I may never hear the patter of their feet but it is good to know I have such a strong son as you to make those things possible.

"Hannah has been calling me. In my sleep I hear her clearly. 'Yitsak,' she says, 'come.' 'My dove,' I answer her, 'what will happen to our Yekele if I come to you?' 'He will be all right, he will be all right,' she keeps repeating as she disappears into the mists.

"Yekele, if I go to her, will you be all right? tell me you will."

"Yes, Papa, I'll be all right. I am big for my age. I can take care of myself, Papa."

"Now let's try to rest and sleep. Tomorrow will be a hard day," urged Yitsak as he pressed his son closer to himself.

The wind seemed to be letting up. Jacob likened the

wind to the cry of a wounded coyote, an angry growl slowly changing into a low moan, a kind of mournful wail almost; then rousing itself again, it howls. . . .

Again Jacob felt his father's arm tighten around him. "Think on the things I just told you, son."

"Yes, Papa, I will."

Jacob did. Over and over again, as they lay there. It was the first time his father had spoken to him like that, man to man. Before he fell asleep, Jacob vowed he'd never forget his father's words.

Twice he awakened in the night and brushed the snow from his own face and ever so lightly from the face of his father who was breathing heavily. The wind was dying, Jacob thought.

Just as the first streaks of light were breaking in the East Jacob awoke the third time. Everything seemed to be eariely quiet. No wind. Not a sound anywhere. He lay there quietly under the arm of his father for a few minutes.

Strange, the absolute silence, he thought. Then it dawned on him: his father was not breathing!

"God in heaven," Jacob cried out in alarm, "O God of Abraham! Papa, Papa! *Tateh!* Speak to me!" He bounded up, then sank to his knees and shook the frozen body of his father. "Papa! No, no! O God, no! It can't be. It can't be. Papa!"

His father's arm was still stretched out in embrace but the unmoving eyes stared into nothingness, lips frozen in a sad, half-smile. Through loud, retching sobs, Jacob pressed his own lips to those of his father stilled in death, now covered with frost. With both his hands he took his father's head and kissed it over and over again.

Half-kneeling, half-sitting, rocking back and forth, he held his father's body tightly to himself, covering it with tears, torrents of tears, hour after hour. Finally, when all his strength was spent, the sun was high in the heavens. He lay down again. He could not cry anymore. He could not think. He could not pray.

How he wanted to pray but words would not come at all. He could only remember his father tearing at his hair when they told him that his mother was dead, so he tore at his own.

Gradually, bit by bit, life began to seep back into his blood, into his paralized limbs. Gently, ever so tenderly he laid his father's body on the snow, the frozen arm still outstretched in fatherly embrace. He covered his father's face with a rumpled handkerchief.

As Jacob sat down, he never felt so alone in his life. The tears still kept coming but no longer the sobs. In truth he was all alone now, just a little boy silently weeping on the endless prairie. . . .

*　　*　　*

One thing was certain. He had to dig a grave. There was no shovel. An axe would have to do. He chipped away at the frozen ground as fast as he could but progress was slow. He sweated. He rested. Sweated and rested. It was dark when he ate some crusts of black bread; gulped some snow for water and laid down to rest. His back ached, his muscles pained but he had dug about ten inches deep.

"It's all right, it's all right, Yekele" he thought his father was whispering. One time it was so real he sat up with a start only to see the motionless form of his father with his hand still frozen in that last embrace. Nothing was stirring, not even the wind. In the vast silence of the heavens a lonely moon appeared bright orange, an almost bloody red. Somewhere in the distance a coyote let out a mournful howl. Jacob tried to fall asleep again but sleep would not come.

He sobbed softly as he remembered. Verenchanka,

their village in the old country where his parents and grandparents lived. They were such a happy family then. His grandpa, *zejda,* was such a lively old fellow, always singing, always smiling: *bubeleh,* grandma, was much more serious and fussed over him by the hour. His raven-haired mother Hannah he remembered clearly: deeply attached to him, she was ever affectionate to him, ever understanding and helpful to him and to his father.

His father? How could he ever forget! He was something very special. The Jewish people of Verenchanka did not call him a *haimisher* for naught: he had a kind of affinity, a rapport with everyone. People felt cozy and warm with him; yes, a *haimisher mensh* who was close to all in their *shtetl,* their village, to both the rich and to the poorest of the poor. Even the non-Jewish *goyim* of Verenchanka loved him. He was at once their brother, their father and, yes, their confessor just as much as their priest was. With his whole being, Jacob loved his father and now, before heaven and the earth, he vowed to be like him no matter where life would lead him in this vast land.

Memories of happy days in Verenchanka came flooding back to him. He was six years old again, eagerly awaiting his birthday when he got two beautiful white rabbits. At all family celebrations, whether at birthdays or anniversaries there was much feasting and singing. No less moving were the religious holidays like *Rosh Hashanah,* (New Year), *Yom Kippur* (Day of Atonement), or the incomparable *Pesach* (Passover). Other religious holidays held him in their spell too.

Strange that these happy memories should come to him now when his heart was brimming with sorrow, Jacob thought. But, then, their's was a praying household. At least four times a day they prayed.

Zejde would become serious though the contentment of a happy spirit still danced in his eyes as he donned the *talis,* the traditional prayer shawl. Together with Papa he would intone the solemn *Shema Yisrael* ("Hear, O Israel. . . .") or one of the three daily prayers, called the *davens.* Each morning after everyone got up they said the traditional but no less touching thanksgiving to God for having "returned to me my soul, which was in Your keeping." *Yes, Papa your soul is now with our God, in His keeping forever. Remember me to God . . . and to Mama, to zejde, to bubeleh.*

Zejde was buried in his *talis.* Should he bury Papa in his? It was somewhere in the bag he carried. But that can wait until the grave is finished, he figured. His heart choked at the thought.

Sleep would not come and the cold was intense. Out in the distance several coyotes joined in a chorus of prolonged, mournful cries. Perhaps they were wolves? He did not know. He was unafraid because, way down deep, he did not really care.

He thought of Verenchanka again. Two years ago after *zejde* and *bubeleh* died, Papa said there was nothing to keep them anymore in the old country. When they left, Mama somehow knew she would never see Verenchanka and the many friends they were leaving behind.

Winnipeg! Their train pulled into the station in the middle of a raging blizzard like the one they just went through. The waiting room was filled with immigrants from all over Europe, Germans, Hungarians, Romanians, the Poles, Russians and, of course, the English. Since it was late evening, most were already settled in for the night on seats, benches and the floor. Mama spread out Papa's coat and her own on the floor. Papa took out his *talis* and began to say his prayers. He said today he would beg God for health, safety and happiness not only for us but also for all these poor people, especially their children. In the dim light the dark lines around his eyes spoke of total exhaustion but he stood there straight and in quiet dignity. Soon some of the people were pointing at him and laughing. Three young men edged towards him through the crowd. "Dirty *Yid,* scum," one snarled at him; another jeered at him in scoffing, unmentionable words. The third spat at him. Even when the spittle struck his face, he kept on praying.

Jacob was bewildered. Why did they do that? He hadn't done anything to hurt them. He was praying for them too. Papa never hurt anyone. Why did they do that to him? That was the only time Jacob saw his father's eyes glisten with tears. After finishing the prayers, he sat down beside Jacob, took his hand into his own and, without a word, squeezed it tightly. After a while he smiled sadly, "Some day, son, you will understand. Some day you will understand." That's all he said. His Mama was crying. Maybe she did not understand either.

Canada! The land of opportunity, the land of promise, Jacob thought bitterly. Hardship, heartaches and death was all that it had given them since they came. And now it had taken away the last one he had held most dear in the whole wide earth.

He must have dozed off a little because a pale sun was high over the naked horizon when he opened his eyes again. He jumped up, in his half sleeping, half-waking trance, took the axe and furiously chipped away at the grave. Hours later he still was not hungry but eat he must, so he took a piece of dried out, frozen beef and gnawed at it. As he looked at his father's motionless body, the arm still frozen in embrace, his stomach knotted not so much in pain as in pangs of piercing sorrow and desolation. When the sobs came again he grimly grabbed the axe and attacked the ever deepening grave.

It must have been midnight when he sat down again, satisfied that a few more hours of work ought to do it. The night was frigid and silent. The whole north was aglow with what his people said were northern lights, shimmering, cascading, billowing and twisting, as if blown by distant winds. The skies tonight are beautiful, no less than breathtaking, Jacob reflected, as he lay down to sleep. They must be welcoming Papa into heaven. . . . Utterly exhausted Jacob fell asleep in an instant.

He awoke in the pale predawn, still tired but more refreshed than he had been for several days. He got to work immediately. Stopping only once, he had to force himself to eat. Only a few more inches deeper and then . . . he dared not think any further.

He would need a marker. There was no wood around so he decided to use the axe handle. With his knife he carved into the hard wood the six-pronged star of David, then lengthwise **Yitsak Bernstein** and, finally, the dates 1828-1889.

It was done! He tried to pray for strength when he emptied his father's pockets but he could not. Mechanically, with trembling hands, he took out his dad's *talis* and the few pitiful possessions he found in his greatcoat: a coin purse, several crumpled bills and passport. He put the latter into his pocket. He kissed the *talis* and gently wrapped it around the neck. It was at that moment that his inner strength, his resolve, completely gave way. He threw himself upon the body of his father; his pent up emotions broke out in torrents of choking sobs, heart wrenching in their intensity.

"Papa, papa, take me with you," he pleaded, "take me, I don't want to live without you. O God of Abraham, Jacob and Isaac, my soul is bleeding, aching to be with him. Have pity, I'm just a poor boy afraid to go on alone . . . Papa, oh papa!"

Over and over again he kissed the frozen face, trying to warm it with his breath, with his hands, with his tears, as if by some miracle he could coax life back into the stilled features. For what seemed like hours he held the head of his father close to himself, moaning softly like a wounded fawn. He did not want to let go but, as peace seeped into his soul, he knew what he must do.

Trying to shake himself out of a trance-like stupor, he gently dragged his father's body toward the grave. Then, with equal gentleness and tenderness, he lowered it, kissed it one last time and covered the face with his red handkerchief and the thick collar of the greatcoat. In covering the body with clumps of earth, big and small, only one desire burned in the conscious recesses of his mind, *May you, O earth, be kind to Papa. Be kind to him. OLEV 'A SHOLEM, UPON HIM BE PEACE.*

OLEV 'A SHOLEM he kept repeating even as he carefully rounded the mound.

After he marked the grave with the axe handle, Jacob recited the *Kaddish,* the Memorial Prayer, one of the most solemn and ancient of all Jewish prayers:

Yisgadal V'Yiskadash Sh'may Rabo . . .
Magnified and sanctified be the name of God throughout the world. . . .

Fortunately, he had learned it two years before but, try as he might, he could not recall the prayer at a parent's graveside. He made up his own:

"Father of heaven, I grieve the loss
of him who lies here bedded away in
mother earth. I loved him dearly be-

cause I am the flesh of his flesh and
because he was so kind to me. He
did not consider too great any sacrifice in my behalf.
May all his acts of kindness never
fade from my memory. I honor him
for his goodness, his piety, service
and mercy. These he has be-
queathed to me; they are better than
any gold or silver.
"Help me, O God, to live like he did,
so that he may ever be declared
blessed for having me for a son.
Glory be to Thee. Amen."

With unbounding determination he picked up his
gunny sack and his father's, and resolutely began to
march away. At twenty paces, he turned around and,
through glistening eyes, saw the inscription on the
axe-handle marker:

Yitsak Bernstein. 1828-1889

He did not turn around again.*

---

*Five years afterwards Jacob tried to find his father's grave: it is
somewhere about forty miles southwest of Whitewood, Sask. He
was unsuccessful. A prairie-fire had swept the region a year before
his search, probably burning the axe-handle monument.

Jacob himself is buried in Saskatoon where I still visit his grave
and, yes, I recite the *kaddish* once a year though not necessarily on
the anniversary of his death.

Going to My First Baby

Transfer!

There it was in big, bold letters which fairly leaped from the paper: **You Are Hereby Assigned As Pastor To The Parish Of** . . . To make it official the Chancery Office's seal (which some priests regularly dub as the K.G.B. seal) was there too.

After serving a year as the cathedral parish's second assistant, I was positively elated. The process of winding down my affairs mostly consisted of throwing away the mountains of junk which I managed to accumulate during those twelve months. The parish bade me farewell with a touching party and a special collection . . . probably figuring that I was broke. (I was).

When D-day arrived, I packed my clothes, books and other sundry items, helter-skelter, into my Buick Roadmaster which I had bought for a hundred bucks. It was a huge, ten year-old car, almost as big as a Sherman tank, which kept breaking down and its tires kept getting flat; so naturally I was broke most of the time. My salary of $75.00 per month barely kept it in repairs.

By 2:00 p.m. I was on my way, singing out of Saskatoon. I used to bellow out those hymns to the Lord. Maybe even the Lord got tired of hearing that raspy voice of mine, because forty miles out, the water gauge light began to twinkle a brilliant red. That meant only one thing: trouble!

Now, my expertise in automotive mechanics equals that of my culinary skills and laundering: when the car breaks down. I open the hood, scratch my head and just stand there like a first rate dope until someone comes along and maybe can figure out what is wrong.

25

This time I am proud to say I spy the trouble: the fan belt is broken — which even a child with 20/40 vision can spot without difficulty.

Nothing to do but to hoof it to the gas station I passed eight miles back. No cars pass by but a man on a horse does. I hold up my thumb, hitch-hiker style. He pauses and turns around. I explain my trouble and he says, "O.K., hop on. Ole Charlie can easily hold us both." It is a huge Belgian work horse almost as wide as my Buick Roadmaster (but certainly much more reliable). I climb on with the man's help, because I would never have made it otherwise . . . like scaling a mountain. In sitting spread-eagle on the horse, I have to do a rather precarious balancing act, for my feet stretch only ten inches on each side of it.

We ride bareback. Either he prefers it that way or else there is no saddle in the world which would fit such a huge horse. As he trots the horse, it seems I will split straight down the middle or at the very least my hip joints will break. Neither prospect holds any appeal to me at the moment but I hang on for dear life to the man in front of me. Images of a skater's split jump and his falling flat on his bottom, still "split", flit through my mind as I ridiculously bounce from side to side, my legs spreading further and further apart with the horse's every step.

We somehow reach the gas station and, fortunately, it has a belt in stock that fits my car. Since my Belgian-horse man is a typical Saskatchewan farmer, kind and considerate to anyone in trouble on the road, he volunteers to take me back to the car. I cringe. My efforts at walking after that *one-way* horseback ride resemble something between a duck waddle and the tottering of a centenarian. The thought of riding back with him sends shivers down whatever is left of my spine!

The coward in me comes out loud and clear as I stall him unashamedly, "Well, sir, I'd hate to put you out. I'll ask the garage-man if he can take me back." I figure a good scheming mind can weasel out of anything.

Not quite. I ask the garage-man. He spits on the floor, chews his wad again a bit and replies matter-of-factly, "Fifteen bucks, 'cause I'd have to close up the station."

I am financially solvent now (from the farewell party) but not all that solvent to throw away fifteen bucks. Besides, who knows what my Roadmaster has up its bonnet till the end of the trip; so better hang on to all the money I can.

Beggars cannot be choosers, Mother used to say. Up the horse again! Sheer agony. Beads of sweat trickle down my forehead despite the brisk cool breeze, but we do get to the car somehow. We both dismount. He dismounts. I fall flat on my face, for my legs completely give way. He picks me up as I try to restore a semblance of dignity proper to my state.

"May I help you put on the fan belt, your reverence?" he asks. Can he ever!! His offer to help is especially welcome as my idea of replacing a fan belt is downright fuzzy.

Always a man of great foresight, I have no wrench in the car, not even an old rusted one, no pliers, no nothing. This time he looks at me rather strangely and throws up his hands. Well, one cannot think of everything!

"Then, do you have a tire iron?" he asks. Ah, sweet smell of success, I have changed enough tires on the Roadmaster to know what a tire iron is and I've got one!

"Yes, I do, it's in the trunk." I take the keys, go around to the back and open the trunk. My word! This time it is my turn to throw up my hands, for now I distinctly remember that the tire iron is tucked away with the spare tire under all the junk at the very back of the trunk and this, indeed, is filled to the brim. Fortunately, the man is still in front of the car, leaning against the grill, smoking a cigarette. I tackle the job bravely. Working furiously and somewhat desperately, I simply throw the stuff on the roadside. After five minutes there is still a lot of stuff left and, since the tire iron is *under* the spare tire, everything has to be cleared out.

Lucky for me, he is still puffing away on his cigarette in front of the car and, I am sure, wondering why is it taking me so long to retrieve a simple tire iron. Yes, he must have concluded that I am answering nature's call and that is why he does not want to embarrass me.

But five minutes is long enough for anyone to fulfill a natural need. He comes to the back of the car and sees the heap of skates, galoshes, clothes, bags and what-not on the roadside. He just grabs his head, shakes it and all he can say is, "me jumpin great grandmaw!" And all I can think of is that he must regard me either as some kind of nut, retarded, stupid or maybe an escaped mental patient, all in that order. I cannot blame him. Well, all of that is not true: I am not an escaped mental patient!

Still, he helps me retrieve the tire iron by lifting the tire with some junk still on it while I grab the elusive tire iron. Then we tackle the job of trying to put on the fan belt. He works the tire iron: I pull with my bare hands on the belt. We sweat, we groan and grunt for ten minutes and, finally, its on!

Whew! I shake his hand to thank him and truly gratefully add, "Sir, all I can say is that you're the gallant knight on his steed."

"Would you run that by me again or better yet, translate it?" he asks quizzically.

28

"Sure," I reply, "you are a kind, a patient and good man, a very good man, sir."

"Naw, t'aint nothing," he sheepishly replies while scratching his head, "jus' tryin' to help out, jus' trying to help out."

As he walks away to his Belgian horse, I could hear him muttering under his breath, "What a nut, what a nut, and stupid too." Then he trots away to wherever he was going.

T'was My Old Kentucky Home

No more breakdowns plagued the rest of my trip. Breathing a sigh of relief and a prayer, I found the rectory and drove into its weedy backyard.

Wish I could say that the rectory was an imposing structure, a manse that could rival any of the stately plantation mansions, ante-bellum Dixie, say, something resembling *Tara* in *Gone With The Wind*. Actually, it was a litte log house, moved from some farm, with siding put over the logs, a three-room affair with peeling paint and cedar shingles on its roof, now also almost bereft of paint — more *Tobacco Road* than *Tara*.

A preliminary tour of the ancient structure left me weeping and laughing at the same time! *So it is not something one would write home about and, in case I do*, I whisper to no one in particular as I survey what is to be my home for some time to come, *I can always refer to it as My Old Kentucky Home*. The expression, basically noncommittal, has a nice respectable ring to it; while not exactly evoking motherhood and apple pies, neither does it tell of a three-room shack by the railroad track. In other words, it nicely camouflages what this parsonage happens to be, including its proximity to the Canadian National Railroad tracks, thank you.

After unloading all my gear from the car, I am in desperate need to relieve myself. The house has no indoor plumbing, only a two-seater in the back lane. Since all the ladies down the block are still working their backyard gardens, I am too embarrassed to go; so I sit there in the house and, like a dummy, crossing and recrossing my legs, I wait for the sun to go down!

Nature, however, is quickly winning out. Shy or not, I must try to sneak into that outhouse without the ladies noticing. Tippy-toeing down the path leading to it, I completely lose my erstwhile composure during the final steps and lunge forward. So far so good . . . but as I am about to open the door, a little kid spies me, waves his hand in welcome and shouts a most congenial, "Hi, Father. Hi, Father!"

Of course, the block full of ladies, straighten up from their work, smile, and wave too! What to do? Quietly beat a silent retreat into the house? Straighten out my hair? Scratch my legs? Or boldly open the outhouse door and walk in? I choose the last. I had to. Let them think: *Ah-ha, Father is going to the toilet!* I still have a phobia of going into outdoor outhouses.

Whoever originally built the residence on the farm must have loved a lot of sunlight, for he had double windows put into every room. That was all right for the farm where houses are miles apart but for town-living it was like living, eating and sleeping in the display-window at Eaton's department store. With the small rooms and all, it seemed like its walls were all glass. I could look into the neighbors' living room and see what kind of a bridge hand each of their guests had. On the other hand, they could see whether or not I made my bed each morning. Every time I changed my underwear I made sure, even at the risk of putting on the shorts backwards (I did this twice too!) when the lights were out. Changing clothes in the middle of main street would have been just as private.

The house had an old telephone, an old vintage type that hung on the dining-room wall, a box-like affair with mouthpiece extending out about six or eight inches. It nearly killed me one night (it sure would have made a zany headline: **Local Pastor Killed by Telephone**): Awakened by desperate knocking at the back door about midnight, I jump out of bed, grab my bathrobe and race through the dining room. POW! Something knocks me on my haunches with the force of Muhammed Ali's upper cut. After the bursting stars, screaming rockets and cannon blasts subside (I swear one can actually see and hear them!), I spy the offending weapon . . . the telephone mouthpiece, still unrepentant and straight-armed!

I learned and learned fast . . . from managing a household, such as it was, to some of the deepest experiences a person can have this side of eternity. Not a few of the latter are recounted in this book. Yes, for five years, t'was my Old Kentucky Home in Saskatchewan and the folk there were simply wonderful, magnificent no less. We laughed. We cried. We worked and prayed together. There was Grey Fox, Black Annie, Bald Eagle, Wise Owl and Red Susanna. I still love them and cannot pass through that countryside without wiping a tear from my eye. I never stop to visit their children and grandchildren because even after all those years, I fear I cannot tear myself away from their flesh and blood, bone of their bone; yet, I know I must, for my work is now in another field.

I do, however, always stop to visit God's green acre near the farm church, a cemetery where so many colorful and dear parishioner-friends are buried. I read the tombstones and say a prayer for each one of them.

Now they are like beautiful memories spun from gossamer thread. They often lifted the burden from my shoulder and helpd me find the sun on the darkest of days. None of them was ever rich in earthly goods but their love showed in various little ways. Many would come to the Eucharistic Liturgy, to Mass, every morning and would bring some cream straight from the farm, a roasted chicken, a freshly baked loaf of bread, homemade butter, a pie or a cake.

Then, we would just sit and talk about all and everything: about their married children far away, about their health, about the hard times of yesteryear. Were the mushrooms out yet? How about the strawberries, or raspberries? How were the crops doing this year? The words of a song put it well: *Those were the days, my friend, we thought they'd never end.*

But end they did for all those old timers. Whenever any of them died, it was like losing part of the family. Well, in a sense it was losing part of the family, our spiritual family. I was their son, they were my parents. When one by one they went to their heavenly home, I missed each of them deeply.

After twenty odd years, I still miss them and feel sorrow in my heart, only now the pain does not hurt as much.

Making Home Brew for a Wedding

The biggest ambition of most Ukrainian parents before they close their eyes in death's sleep is to marry off their sons and daughters. They know that each son and daughter will have someone to care for, someone to love, a nest to call home and a family of their own. This is considered an immense blessing, worthy of the deepest thanks to God. In their minds as long as their children remain unmarried, they are vulnerable to the world about them. As single people they may be susceptible despite a good Christian upbringing: the world will still try to mold them, to shape them to its own image and, then, throw them away like broken dolls.

Ivan and Anastasia were no exception; if anything, they attached greater importance to having their children married than most Ukrainian parents, for they too equated good, solid Christian marriage with happiness and contentment, with the wholeness of a person. I am glad to say that before the bell tolled at their funerals they saw thirteen of their brood married happily. Only one was still single.

Before the marriage of each, they would call in the prospective son- or daughter-in-law and say, "Now you will become our own child. We will worry about you like your own parents. If you have troubles, trust us as you would your own mother and dad. Our's may not be the best of families but it is good. We will care about you and you will find that we love you, for you are one of our own."

So Liz, the second youngest, was getting married! Despite the number of children in the family, the marriage of each was unique and they tried to make it as nice, as memorable as possible. They did too.

They had retired into the village but still kept their old homestead. The mother had her work to do for the wedding; the father, his. Hers was to prepare the food: the hundreds of *perohy* (dumplings), *holuptsi* (cabbage-rolls), the sausages, hams, the roasts. His job, first of all was, to kill the fattened calf and pig, and help all he could in general, but in particular his job was to make enough home-brew so that the guests would have plenty to drink, usually about thirteen to fifteen gallons of it. One may think that was a lot but, considering how huge was each side of the clan, how numerous their neighbours and friends, it was not all that excessive. Well, it was a lot but that was quite a bit of wine, too, that Christ changed from water at Cana of Galilee . . . about a hundred and twenty gallons . . . especially when one remembers that it, too, was a village.

I did not know how to make home-brew. Since I have never seen it done, I was curious. So I asked sixty-eight year Old Ivan if he would allow me to come and see. Besides, he needed help in carrying the cold water from the well to the still.

We get up at half past four in the morning and drive out to the old homstead.

"But you know, Sir, if the mounties come to raid us, I'll cop out and say that as your pastor I've come to admonish you, to persuade you not to do it. And you will have to back me up on it."

"Sure, don't worry, Fadder (Father), I is gonna tell them that."

So we begin. In all seriousness, he first takes off his cap, bows, and makes the sign of the cross in order to dedicate every work to God, just as he was taught in the old country.

I chuckle all day as I remember that respectful, sincere sign of the cross. Well, the depths of faith can never be fathomed, but *I betcha, God, You've never had the distilling of home-brew ever dedicated to Your honor and glory and in such a serious way!*

We sweat all day, carrying the cold water, the wood for the fire and other sundry tasks to make the best sixteen gallons this side of Swan River.

The RCMP did not raid us. At seven in the evening we finish, weary but satisfied with our handiwork.

We sit down on stumps of wood, like grimy cowpokes, man to man, I and my Ukrainian friend (he is by now much more than my parishioner, for all through the day we have been sampling each batch brewed).

Then he takes the jug again, pours some of Saskatchewan's best, makes the sign of the cross very reverently in thanksgiving and says, "Friend, *daj Boze*" (literally, *God grant*, with the words grant you *happiness, health* or whatever being understood).

"*Daj Boze*, friend."

From then on I knew that I, a "foreign" young priest, was accepted among the Ukrainians, for I had shared the making of home-brew with one of their patriarchs. I was "on their side," one of them now, for he trusted me completely!

No greater trust hath man than . . . Ask the RCMP!

Shakespeare, You Were So Right!

Romeo and Juliet on the endless prairies of Saskatchewan! Perhaps the people of the prairies whether in Texas, Oklahoma, Kansas or Nebraska who have often known the pathos of loneliness and sadness will understand this tragedy better than most.

They were two young people, Bohdan and Maria, healthy, full of life. They were in love, a tender sensitive love, something like Lara and Yuri in Boris Pasternak's *Doctor Zhivago* . . . frolicking in the grassy meadows, romping in the mown hayfields and merrily wrestling each other in the barn.

Their parents at first were not concerned at all. Young people are young besides, they, the parents, were too busy working the endless fields, tending the livestock and in general trying to feed their brood. They hardly noticed the antics of Bohdan and Maria.

The glory of loving someone and being loved in return! For the first time in their short lives they experienced love and they were overwhelmed. Like all couples in love, they thought their's was a unique love, one of a kind in the whole wide world, sensitive, beautiful and intense. They did not mind if the whole world knew.

In one of their weaker moments, despite themselves, they sinned, passionately but honestly. Those were the very words they used. She became pregnant.

Their great love for each other did not change one whit but the parents, instead of trying to understand, could not be restrained in their anger and injured pride, as if an evil spirit entered into them. Maybe it did.

"Your worthless son ruined our innocent daughter; it's his fault, "accused the irate parents of Maria.

"It's your daughter, she was the one who seduced our good son," argued the parents of Bohdan.

The feud was on.

After weeks of venomous family recriminations and counter-recriminations, Bohdan and Maria were hurting. They did not want to harm anyone, least of all their parents. But they knew, they would never be able to marry each other, be husband and wife. Their parents made that very clear. But they knew or so they thought, they could never live apart, be without each other for life. The empty loneliness of life without one another was too much for them to bear . . .

They found them in the haybarn. They drank gopher poison, one of the most painful ways to die, probably the only way they knew. They died embracing, cheek to cheek, their tears still wet on their faces now rapidly growing cold. I was called. I was there.

With all the powers of my priesthood, I absolved them from every sin and gave them the last anointing. I thought they were right with God, no matter what.

Then I stooped and kissed both of them. "My children," I could not help saying aloud, "You did not honestly think that you sinned, I'm sure. Certainly you were the ones who were greatly sinned against. God understands. He loves you both, much, much more than you loved each other."

Then I went out and vomited.

After the funeral the families came together, drawn by their common grief. They finally understood why it happened. They are still friends and visit each other.

O God, why not before. Why not before?

Why, Lord, Why?

When Mehmet Ali Agca shot Pope John Paul II, the Holy Father could not believe it, "*Perche l'hanno fatto*, Why did they do it," he asked as he crumbled and collapsed into the arms of his aide.

On hearing the news a man in Israel, a good man, sobbed, "It's like shooting God!"

Well, it was.

George Bernard Shaw put it well when he wrote after the assassination of Mahatma Gandhi, "It shows how dangerous it is to be good."

Many times, in many places, people have asked why they and others, especially the good, have to suffer.

Often physical pain and suffering are easier to bear than inner turmoil and agony. Here again it is the very best who suffer the most. Anyone who does not care, who is not sensitive to the needs or welfare of others will not bleed in anguish. In any command, in any position of authority great or small, the truly good will feel the same most of the time: helpless, torn and crucified.

Take any honorable military officer, for example, a paratrooper, who must control his emotions and give orders, knowing that hundreds of men will die. *My God*, he thinks in his heart, *how can I do it? My decision may be wrong*, he agonizes, *but my indecision may be worse in the long-run.*

As an upright man, however, he knows he has to do it because later even many, many more lives may be lost. So mustering up all the courage he can command, he shows no emotion when he conducts the briefing, and crisply, matter of factly says, "One hundred men jump tonight." In his heart he knows that, despite favorable intelligence reports, many of his men will be dead by 0900 hours. Part of his heart dies with every word, in fact, with every step he takes as he marches smartly back to his quarters, closes the door . . . and sometimes weeps in his desolation. His outward manner seems unfeeling, mechanical, almost machine-like but inwardly his soul bleeds. Machines do not weep, they do not bleed. Nor do machines ask questions as the paratrooper does of himself: why should these men jump and die? Yes, why should they? Why should they suffer from wounds for days or months? Why should they be maimed for a lifetime? Why did it happen to them and not me?

The painful questions may last for a few days or for a lifetime, as they did for Colonel Brown (USAAF, ret.) who came hundreds of miles from the U.S.A. to see me in Saskatchewan. Since his wife died, the questions started again. He was a changed man from the Colonel who had fought over the skies of Europe during World War II.

That was in another world, in another age. One cannot say that he was a broken man, only sad, profoundly sad.

It was a sunny afternoon in the last part of August when we went out for a walk around a huge field of wheat undulating in the cool breeze. His pace was brisk, his bearing military, almost parade-ground perfect. There was a slight stoop to the shoulders, hardly detectable if one were not observant.

"It was a bright day like today, Kaz, when I almost bought it in '44," he began. "It was supposed to be a milk-run. Some milk-run with enemy planes zeroing in from every direction.

"The initial shock was intensified by the bedlam banging through the interphone system. Nearly everyone in the crew saw and tried to report enemy fighters from all points of the compass. I was furious: furious at myself for being surprised and furious at my crew for breaching discipline. I cursed them profanely, urging absolute silence for we could survive only if they remained calm, disciplined and efficient.

"Naturally, silence was to be broken only when absolutely necessary. Ominous reports, however, kept pouring through the intercom: from the tail gunner, 'Bogies at six o'clock climbing (meaning climbing to the rear of the bomber) . . . more coming at six o'clock high' (more coming from high above, again to the rear of the plane); from the port waist gunner, 'Colonel, bandits at nine o'clock direct' (off the left wing); from the dorsal gunner, 'look, at three o'clock too.'

"I myself saw others coming from twelve o'clock, some streaming directly towards the nose of the plane. I warned the crew of imminent bandits from all points but forbade wasting ammunition on any fighters out of range.

"Then all hell broke loose. Thirty seconds seemed like an hour. First wave. It was like being in the middle of an angry swarm of bees. And this was supposed to be a damned milk-run!

"The second wave followed almost immediately . . . from all quarters again! Their timing was perfect, their technique masterly, finely co-ordinated, one of their finest. Their 20 mn. cannons were piercing our plane like hail through tin foil."

The colonel never liked to talk about his wartime experiences but now his words came flooding out like water from a bursting dam. He was a helpless child now, I reflected, no longer the master, no longer the iron disciplinarian at whose words better men than I used to quake. Pouring out those deadly moments of combat from his soul may serve as a kind of catharsis, I decided; so I did not interrupt.

"Through the bedlam I was cursing the crew again for wasting ammunition. It was a long way home yet. I looked about in every direction, my face against the ice-cold window. Bandits all over the place! Two Fortresses fell out of formation, wobbling out of the box.

Suddenly, the cockpit seems to compress on me, like being trapped within a cage of steel, glass, controls and clusters of instruments. Over the din I hear the tail gunner's voice, from somewhere far away, 'My guts are falling out, Colonel, my guts are falling out!'

"My next words? I cannot forget them. Maybe because it was Nebraska, as we used to call him, or maybe it was because of the dream I had the night before. I don't know. I've said similar words to others quite a few times, more than I care to remember, but somehow every word is seared into my memory: 'Pilot to tail gunner. Pilot to tail gunner. Help is on the way,' I lied, 'hang in there, son!'

"His voice, fainter by the second, still reports, 'Ahh . . . seven o'clock high . . . twin engines . . . ow-w . . . Jesus, rockets . . .' and his voice trails off.

"Angry, shapeless blobs of red flame streak in. Many find their mark, sounding like someone throwing stones, huge stones, against a tin roof of a tool-shed back on the farm.

"An explosion of glass splinters and iron! The wind rushes in with tornado force. The Fort shakes, shudders, almost groaning in its death throes. A jagged tear appears in its wing. I tell the crew to bail out. The wing folds upward in slow motion. I stare at it in disbelieving fascination. Only for a second. In jumping out of the seat, I see Paul, my co-pilot. Only the bottom jaw is left where his head used to be. The fuselage opens like an eggshell and I fall out. Then, the explosion. That is it. I forget to pull the rip cord until I see another chute open. None of the others made it. G-forces? Wounds? Dead?

"As I flow to earth and PW camp I wonder WHY? They were good men, excellent men. All my buddies, gone. Why did they have to die? Why not me? An overwhelming sense of guilt hits me for having survived. Yes, why them and not me?"

Years later the Colonel still wonders why. He came hundreds of miles from the U.S.A. to see me in Saskatchewan to find out if he could get a partial answer at least. He seemed to be a tortured soul.

"Why did my men, my friends, have to die, Father? Why? I feel so dirty, so guilty to have survived. You and General George Schulgen (USAAF) were very close friends, Father, did you ever talk about such things?"

"No, Colonel, we never talked about such things because too many of his friends died too, not only in the War but in peace time accidents. When he joined the U.S. Air Force in 1924 it was only eight hundred strong. As the years went by, one by one they died. When he retired in 1948 there were only eight of the originals left. No, we never talked about why so many of his friends died."

We stop under an old oak and sit down on the grass for a cigarette. The Colonel's hand shakes as he lights up. Beads of sweat glisten on his forehead despite the coolness of the breeze. He had fought many air battles prior to that last one. Perhaps all of them coalesced into that personal Armageddon which he just relived so intensely.

"To tell you the truth, Colonel, I don't know. I really don't. I'm just a poor Saskatchewan priest, but listen, Sir, I'm convinced that there is an answer though we may never find it this side of the grave. I don't hold up any banners, nor mouth any glib slogans or platitudes. And I will never say that there is a silver lining to your cloud of pain.

"Nor will I ever say that it is God's will. No, Sir, it's not. God is not a monster or some Aztec deity demanding human life. Philosophers have grappled with the problem of suffering and death for centuries; so did the theologians. None have come up with any really satisfactory answers.

"All we know is that God gave human beings free will and He will never take it away.

"Why did He give free will? So that people can love Him. Simple as that. You have to have free will to truly love. A forced love is no love. It's worth thinking about. Unfortunately, all of us abuse free will when we sin. Some greatly, others in a little way.

When people choose to inflict pain whether in war or murder, in heartbreak or betrayal, God will never step in to take away their free will in order to stop them.

"Of one thing I'm sure, Colonel, you should never feel guilty about your survival or the deaths of your men. You did your job honorably and capably. So why should you feel guilty? Use the rest of your life well. Maybe that's why you survived. You can still do a lot of good in this world.

"Look, as a priest, an officer of God, I've had to make many decisions affecting thousands of souls for time and eternity. I made these decisions the best way I knew how and the rest I left to God. I can't sit on my hands and be indecisive. That, too, may affect souls adversely. I can't worry about my past decisions or I would end up in a strait jacket.

"That is one thing General Schulgen taught me, a lesson I really took to heart. Hope you can too, Sir.

That was fifteen years ago. Since then the Colonel

has been devoting his life, full time, working with ex-cons and dope addicts on Chicago's south side.

Going to Town

Through the years, Saskatchewan did itself proud in road building. The province has forty-three per cent of Canada's highways, though it has less than five percent of the nation's population. Twenty-five years ago the quality of those roads was something else. Most of the farm roads were nothing more than bare earth which became a gooey, sticky mud or gumbo whenever it rained. A vehicle, any vehicle, would slither and slide regardless of the driver's skill or expertise. It was always a matter of luck whether one got stuck in the mud or slid into a ditch.

Mr. and Mrs. Buk were typical Ukrainian old-timers. He, with handlebar mustache, wide suspenders, was the epitome of manliness; today we'd call him *macho* in no uncertain terms. She was a buxom, heavy set woman, working right beside him in the fields, barn or stable. Their family was grown up and scattered over Canada, but her motherly instincts still showered care on anyone's son or daughter, young or old. "*Dytyno,* child," she would say, "here, let me sew on that button for you," or "here is a nice piece of buttered bread for you." Always caring, always solicitous.

Jeez, I laughed when I heard it! It was after one of those typical Saskatchewan downpours that they had to go into town for groceries. Here he was, sitting straight as an arrow, steering the Model A Ford, pride of his life, but by now splattered with mud and gumbo. Old man Buk was a marginal driver under the best of circumstances, but in this mud, forget it. He was game, however, honor personified, even in this situation. I had driven that road many times during wet weather and it was tricky. When coming to a downhill and seeing a mud puddle at the bottom one really does not know whether the ruts are passable or not. Brazen it out and hope for the best? He did.

There it is, down a slight slope, a puddle. By golly, werr-rre, werr-rrer, woff! Stuck in the mud! They look at one another. Here is *macho* personified, his innate gentleness and kindness towards "his woman" urges him to go out and push the car but, of course, she does not know how to drive (nearly all the immigrant Ukrainian women do not drive).

Without saying a word, they both know it: they are stuck, it is a fact. Knowing what must be done, she goes out, bundles up her voluminous skirts and HEAVE HO! The Volga Boatmen, all over again. Of course, he presses the gas-pedal, now called the accelerator, and the wheels spin, splattering mud all over her, her clothes, hands and face (her shoes had already sunk in the mud; she could feel the water squishing between her toes).

Heave-ho, heave-ho. Once more. *Heave-ho.* One more push should do it. Yep, the car is slowly crawling up onto higher ground. Old Buk — I know the feeling — does not want to stop until he is sure he will not get stuck again. Sometimes that can be up to a quarter of a mile. She knows that, too, so she is not concerned at first.

But he is not stopping! *Holera* (literally, *cholera*, the closest a pious Slav usually comes to swearing), he has forgotten about her! Old Buk, utterly relieved that he is out of the mud, completely forgets about his wife and goes into town alone! Only then does he think about her!

Later on she told me, "When he forgot about me, I raised my fist to heaven and even tried to curse him but then I thought, *He's my man, he really does love me in his own way, the bull. I understand him and,*

50

after all, he is somebody's son." Then she added, "Hey, Fadder, do you understand?"

"Yes, Mrs. Buk I understand. And your love is beautiful."

The last time I saw Mr. and Mrs. Buk was about fifteen years ago at their fifty-fifth wedding anniversary and, the beauty of it is, they still "understand and love" each other in their own but very real way.

Dressing Up To Receive Christ

After being a priest for several years, I was pastor of a district which included ten mission "parishes".

In one of these "parishes" up North, I came across a man who had been away from the sacraments for quite a number of years. He really could not get to the nearest church, as he was in his eighties, did not own a car, and the church was at least five miles away. He lived alone in a one-room hut, better described as a summer kitchen (where, in summer, meals are cooked and eaten, a separate building from the farm house).

Everything about the place was neglected, grimy and in disarray. I blessed his home and told him I would be glad to return the next day, hear his confession and give him Christ in the Eucharist. He was glad to have a chance to square himself with God and receive Christ.

Next day, he opened the door and invited me in. The rough boards of the floor were scrubbed clean — no mean task for a man in his eighties — even his clothes were hung on nails in the room. Other articles were piled into one corner, his bed was made and, in general, one could see he must have worked for half the night. After I remarked how nice the house looked, he simply said: "After all, Fadder, I want to receive Christ as nicely as possible!"

What I found really touching was that, despite his overalls being the same he wore the day before, he really must have done his best to launder them by hand in the galvanized washtub still standing by his bed. They were probably the best he had. But instead of the checkered shirt, he had worn the day before, he put on a white one, clean though badly in need of ironing. Still, I thought *God bless you, Petro, you really are trying to receive Christ as nicely as possible and in what is to you your Sunday best.* And he was positively beaming with pride.

Christ must have smiled as he came into the heart of this lonely, sincere, old man that day. I know I did, reverently and affectionately. Jesus was a poor man, too, so He would naturally understand another poor man.

How Great Thou Art. How Great Thou Art, O God, to come to your lowly servants. Driving down the bush-road, I recalled not without great emotion another lowly, old servant of God in another place, in another country. Originally from Poland, he owned a mill in the hills. At seventy seven he had to have both legs amputated because of frostbite. At the mill two years later he was slowly dying. The nearest priest? Forty miles away! His wife, not much younger than he, hurriedly walked the distance to get a priest.

Alone in bed while she was away, the old Mazowiec (a man from the region of Central Poland where Warsaw is situated) prayed and prayed. Knowing his strength was ebbing away, he longed for his Christ in the Eucharist — intensely, yearningly. On the third day, his hope gave way. *The priest will never come with the sacraments,* he thought. *He would have been here by now. Perhaps, God is punishing me because of some great sin I have done in my life. Come Christ, my strength is going, Come Christ, please.*

Suddenly the door opens and the priest hurries in. In his great joy, the old Mazowiec calls out, *"Jezu, Jezu ty przyszed, ty przyszed do mnie" (My Jezu, Jezu, You came to me, You came to me).* Forgetting he had no legs, impulsively he tried to run to greet the priest carrying Communion. He falls flat on his face but still from the floor he sobs plaintively, "*Jezu, Ty przyszed* . . . Jezu, You came."

The priest absolves him, places the sacred host on his lips and anoints him. Only then do the wife and priest pick up the old miller and put him to bed. Tearfully, he recounts his intense yearning and his doubts of the previous three days. Then he closes his eyes and drifts into a semi-coma, mournfully repeating, "Jezu, You came to me."

Those were his last words. He died at four o'clock in the morning.

How Great Thou Art, How Great Thou Art, O God to come to your lowly servants!

Who is the Saint, Who the Sinner?

Old Nick for years was the number-one Communist in his community. I thought I had him for Christ, but that was one I lost.

No fault of mine. Excuses? No, I do not think so. It happened this way.

I met him at a house-warming party at his neighbor's, my parishioners. My Ukrainians called it a *warm-house* party! It was about five o'clock in the afternoon when I arrived. After driving about two hundred and fifty miles between Sunday Liturgies with nothing to eat since midnight, I was really hungry. The pre-Vatican Two Catholic Church was very strict about pre-Communion fasting: a few drops of water, or a bite of food after midnight would break the Eucharistic fast. Church legislators then did not scruple to ruin a man's health to uphold their **Sacred Law.** And I was dumb enough to obey every letter of that **Law. Law** was **Law** to me then.

Anyway, at "the warm-house party" I happened to sit by this kindly, jolly white haired man of about eighty. He told me, his name was Nick. After a couple of drinks of "home-brew," he really warmed up and we talked about many things.

He knocked about the world in his day. Of some things he had done, he was proud. Of other things he was ashamed. He remembered how he used to go to church in the old country with his mother and dad, and he used to know almost all the church services by heart. As a kid he used to go to confession and Communion faithfully every Christmas and Easter and felt good about being forgiven all his sins. He was especially proud to be able to sing the old Ukrainian hymns and carols right alongside his dad even at home. They lived in a two-room hut. Because of the lack of room, his parents slept in one bed; he and his sister in another.

The year he was nine, he had been told by a schoolmate, also a nine year old, that it was not right to sleep with a female, a sin no less. He took it to heart and in his Easter confession he told the priest that he "slept with his sister."

"Son," the priest scolded in a voice loud enough to be heard in the whole church, "that is a terrible sin! You must never do it again or you will go to hell. Now stay on your knees through the whole of Vesper Service and beg God's forgiveness. Maybe He'll never forgive you."

Nick could see God driving him to the fires of hell and sealing his fate there forever and ever. All through Vesper Service he sweated and cried.

When he got older he understood what could have happened by sleeping with a female, even one's sister, but at the time he had no idea. What could have been so terribly wrong about it, he wondered. After all, he thought it was a much bigger sin to get angry with the family geese which he had to watch and pasture.

"That was about seventy two years ago and I haven't gone to confession since," he said. "If God was such a tyrant I wanted no part of him. A decade after that confession I met some Bolsheviks who were understanding and tried to help people in every way. I became one of them. For all these many years I worked with them, trying to organize the masses to better their lot.

"Now Father, I am old and much wiser. I think about God every day and would like to go to church again and, yes, to confession and to receive Jesus in

Communion again because despite everything I still believe in Him. You seem, Father, to be understanding just like the Bolsheviks I worked with and if you can help me with this I'll be grateful to the end of my days. Can you do it, Father?

"Sure, Nick, anytime. Come to church on Sunday and we will take care of it. Believe me, we will."

Nick did come. You could see in his radiantly happy eyes, that he was genuinely moved to come back to the God he left so long ago.

After the Eucharistic Liturgy Nick came down the steps of the church. Not a word of welcome from anyone in the congregation, just an opppressive silence. The silence was suddenly broken by the booming voice of a long-standing Catholic, one of those righteous ones, who feel they have to "protect" God and His church: "Nick, what is a Bolshevik like you doing here? You should be ashamed of yourself."

Ashamed, heart-broken, tears streaming down his face, Old Nick hastened to his car. He was hurting, hurting deeply.

That evening I went to his house to see him. Subdued, he received me quietly but very kindly. You could see the deep hurt etched in the deep, somber lines of his face. Only a half day passed but the change in Old Nick was palpable. My words of comfort seemed only to increase the heaviness of his sadness, a sadness that no man could take away, only God.

As I went back to the car to drive the ten miles back to the rectory, he came out and grasped my hand, "Go with God, Father. Maybe someday people will be different, your people and my people. Maybe they will forgive and love one another. Go with God."

He never set foot in a Catholic Church again, but I am convinced that God must have embraced Old Nick when he came to Him in death five years later. I still often think of him and pray for him and ask him to pray for me.

Who is the sinner, who the saint?

Maybe someday, Nick, people will forgive and love one another, your people and my people. I know we did — A Communist and a priest!

Joey's Best Friend

The dog was only a spotted, shaggy mongrel but a boy and his dog were never more inseparable. Wherever Joey went, Tiger was sure to be at his side.

Together they used to go to bring the cows home from pasture. Many a time Joey would open the gate and Tiger would bring in the cattle by himself. Sometimes Joey would help Tiger round up the herd and head it for home, with Tiger trotting happily behind him. At other times Tiger, with tongue hanging out, tail wagging, would scamper behind the cattle; he would dart from side to side of the herd, hurry the stragglers and, in general, would keep the herd together.

On lazy afternoons, they would sit under an old poplar in the yard. Joey would talk to Tiger, stretch out and fall asleep with his hand still on Tiger's head. Often Tiger would pretend to be dozing but, actually he was looking at Joey through half-closed eyes, filled with adulation and affection.

Joey taught Tiger many tricks: walking on his hind legs; jumping through hula-hoops; flying a kite with Tiger holding the string in his mouth; all sorts of things with which they entertained the neighboring children.

Best of all, they loved to go fishing, just the two of them. Invariably, Joey would sit on the shore, fish-line in the water while Tiger would nap or else sniff around trying to scare out a wild duck or a rabbit.

On his ninth birthday Joey got sick. There was a finality about it. Diagnosis? Leukemia! When they brought Joey home he lingered just over six weeks. Tiger never wanted to leave Joey's side in the sickroom. Most of the time he just gazed at Joey with his big brown eyes — always it seemed they were too big for a dog like that. When the end of Joey's life was drawing to a close, Tiger must have sensed it: his big brown eyes not only lost their sparkle but they became almost human-like in their piteous sadness. The time came when Joey was too weak to lift his hand to pet Tiger on the head. It was then that Tiger would snuggle his nose under Joey's hand and softly whimper.

At Joey's wake, which in those days was generally held in the house of the deceased, and at his funeral, everyone forgot about Tiger. Joey was buried in the family plot beside his grandpa and grandma, about twenty miles away.

After the funeral someone remembered about Tiger but he was nowhere to be seen. A month later they found Tiger, now also dead, at the grave of Joey. They figured he starved to death by that grave. He was lying on his stomach, head between his front paws as if staring at the little mound of earth beneath which his friend was buried.

Now, both of them are resting side by side in that lonely prairie cemetery. The family wanted it that way. The epitaph reads:

> Here Rest Our Joey and His Best Friend Tiger
> May They Be Happy Together Again

A Funeral

Rain and snow. Rain and snow! There would be no sun for his funeral.

His name was Max. Lord, he was a good man. Maybe he did sin but he was good, really good, down deep. He could never stop his tears over a sick child, anybody's child. He knew what sickness-suffering was, having experienced it himself many times.

Later in life, at great sacrifice, he never refused to take people, strangers or not, to the sickbed of a loved one, sometimes over sixty miles of rutted, prairie roads.

The poor? Max, he always had a soft spot for the needy. His whole heart was soft and went out to anyone too poor to afford to eat. He shared his bread and milk with others when, during the nineteen thirties, he himself literally had nothing more to give except his love and concern. Love and concern always went with the bread he shared.

Yes, he was full of life too. He could dance his life away. Well, maybe not his life, but at least his troubles, his sorrows. Yes, as an elderly man, he told me himself that he loved women, that he appreciated God's gift to men and he meant it. Before he got married, he said, he sinned with them many times. That is why he got married at eighteen back in 1924.

Full of life, he wanted the sun for his funeral but, no, the rain and snow kept coming down in ever greater torrents across the Saskatchewan, wind-swept prairie as his funeral procession wound its way around the sloughs to the small country cemetery where he wanted to be buried beside his first wife.

His first wife? More than half his life went out of him when she died. You could see it in the tears that glistened in his eyes whenever he talked about her after she was gone. He really never got over the shock, not really. He started drinking heavily after the funeral, probably to deaden the pain.

Then he went to his childhood sweetheart, also widowed; the first time in a stupor of liquor. He was trying to find some of the love his first wife had given him. The widow accepted the widower and they were married in six weeks! His children, relatives and friends were horrified. He is destroying himself, they said. Maybe he was. To the depths of his being he regretted the day he married his second wife. That was the first time I got to know Max.

Now five years later, about thirty cars filled with all his friends, relatives, and neighbors sloshed their way to bury him in God's little acre by the church along that lonely, dirt road past his former farmhouse.

The house had known the sound and laughter of his first wife and his eleven children but today, through its broken windows, it heard only the sound of wind, snow and rain . . . and the tears of those who loved him. Total desolation. Only those who have lived on the endless, open prairies know the forlorn lonesomeness that such a scene evokes. Prairie people cling to one another to survive, to remain sane, or to avoid taking to the bottle. Probably that is why they are so ready and willing to talk to anyone, to perfect strangers even, when riding the bus, the train or the plane. Mere friendliness cannot explain this fact.

Anyway, seeing that frame farmhouse, during the funeral procession of this grand ole man who loved God and people, through my tears — because I understood and cherished him — I thought, *dear Max, it sums up your life, this old house of yours on the prairie, good times and bad, happy and sad times. You sure had them.*

We got further on. The rain stopped but the snow kept coming down in billowy waves of white. We could hardly see the road. Prairie weather, one minute good, the other bad. *Hey, Max, I'm sure you are with God now. You lived on these prairies most of your life, so maybe you even ordered this weather. After all, whether in tragedy or in happiness you lived through all kinds of weather, through all kinds of storms and you didn't even mind blizzards when you knew you had enough provisions to feed your family. Maybe you ordered this weather because it was so much a part of your life.*

We turned the corner for the last four miles to St. Stanislaus, the Polish Cemetery, beside the little wooden church of the same name. Like Max's farmhouse, the church too is abandoned now. Holy Mass had not been celebrated there for about ten years because of lack of priests. This Max could not understand. More sadness. In his final years, he would take me there and wonder why it was so.

Ole Max and many of his neighbors were the ones who, at great sacrifice to themselves, had built the wooden church. Whenever we were going up there he would say, "I wonder, Father, if the birds still stay and nest under its eaves as they used to. Is that cross still standing straight on its steeple?" Just by looking at him I knew it was one of the most important things in his life.

And I would say, "Yes, Max, there are birds still nestling under its eaves, and the cross is still straight on its steeple. And yes, the lilies are still growing by its sides."

First we would mend the fence and cut the grass by the church and on the cemetery. We would finish by pulling out all the weeds from around the lilies. Max would feel proud and happy. "All right, then, let's go back to town for some coffee and lunch," he would say, "but first let's go and pray by the grave of my wife."

As his funeral procession rounded the last slough near St. Stanislaus, I saw it: the cross on the steeple was leaning to one side! *But Max*, I thought, *look the church is still standing.* As I was driving with the hearse, I put my hand on his coffin and through the tears whispered, "and, friend, you yourself know that the lilies don't bloom at this time of year. You know that. The birds? Well, most flew South weeks ago. I'm sorry."

Slowly, yet somehow magestically, the hearse turned into the cemetery and on through the tall grass now bent low under the load of snow. Max was the last one to cut the grass but that was five months previously, in early June, just before his final illness.

The snow let up. The hearse stopped. One could see the tombstones clearly now: his first wife's, his parents', his two little sons', his neighbors' and friends' of yesteryear. He used to tell me about them, great things and small, humorous things and sorrowful. He loved them and missed them deeply when they died. But Max used to put it differently — that they went to the Lord.

My mind was not on the burial prayers. I kept looking at those tombstones and the loved ones they represented. It seemed all of them were there to greet him now, to welcome him forever.

Death is not the end of life, it is only a separation, a separation filled with tears. I believe that, Max, to the core of my being. You used to say that, too, my friend.

When the funeral prayers ended, I took the lily, a tiger-lily, Saskatchewan's flower, now lifeless and faded, pressed between the pages of my prayer-book, looked at it and put it on his coffin.

I raised my eyes towards the sky to breathe a final

little prayer for his soul and there they were — two snow birds circling, flying lower and lower around all of us!

Yes, Max, the lilies are still blooming and, friend, the birds will nestle under the eaves of our little church tonight, just as you always wanted!

You Bleed, I Bleed

His parishioners called him "the whiskey priest." He had been a chaplain in the Canadian infantry during World War II. After the war, he was assigned as pastor of two small country parishes. For him, however, the war never went away, not really, until the day he himself died.

I do not know, maybe the War was just an excuse for his drinking. Other chaplains, after all, went through similar hells of war, yet readjusted well afterwards. Perhaps psychiatrists can explain. I cannot.

When he was dying of cirrhosis of the liver, he told me many of his experiences and it was always war, the utter horrors of it and what it was like. He simply could not let go of what most soldiers want to forget.

"Look, Father," he would say, "in war, there are no good days even if your side is winning. There are only bad days because of the killing and maiming. Sure, maybe not that day or the day before, maybe not even a week before but the wounded are still suffering and dying everyday."

I would answer, "Don't torture yourself anymore, George. You have suffered too much already."

Most of the time wincing, whether from the recollections or whether from physical pain, it was hard to tell, but George would always go on, "Yes, Father, I don't know how many dying men I've attended. It must have been in the hundreds though."

"George, do yourself a favor, don't torture yourself anymore, please."

He would not stop, however, "I still can see those eyes of the wounded, pleading to tell them that they are not dying. I don't think I was lying when I told them, 'Listen, it's going to be all right, it's going to be all right.' But how could they be all right with the stomach shot out, bullets through their lungs, without legs . . . You name it.

"After a while you get a sixth sense even about those whose wounds do not seem fatal. It was always the same whether in bombing raids, in attacks when a man can be cut in half almost faster than you can blink your eye, or later in the field stations.

"The Catholics I'd absolve, *'ego te absolvo ab omnis peccatis tuis . . . I absolve you from all your sins . . .*

"Most needed reassurance: 'Yes, son, all your sins are forgiven now. Would you like to receive Christ in Holy Communion? Good.' I would place the host on their tongue and we would pray together in our own words. Sometimes the host would be tinged with the soldier's own blood streaming from his mouth, his blood mingling with Christ's Own. God!

"In praying with the non-Catholics, again using our own words, I'd stress sorrow for sin and love for Christ. Many times we would keep repeating the Lord's Prayer or the beautiful Psalm, *The Lord is my shepherd, I shall not want . . .*

"I would always make it a point to hold the dying soldier's hand. When the death rattle came, I would squeeze it, to show I was still there, that somebody cared very much. Many times I had to look away, I just had to, so my tears wouldn't show if by chance he could still see, because it would only add to his pain.

"I'll never forget during an especially savage artillary barrage in the predawn near Caen. The noise was deafening, the dark was being pierced by quick flashes of light, like lightning in a fierce electrical storm, and the ground was shaking. I could hardly hear it, a voice desperately calling for help. I strained to hear from which direction. Yes, there it was again, 'Padre, padre,

Mother of God, help me, help me. I don't want to die, I don't want to die. Help me, help me.'

"So I crawl. No, I really do not know how I got there. If you are the Padre, you run, crawl, you claw the earth, you eat dirt. You do anything. All you know is that a soldier needs you.

"I never cared whether the soldier was Protestant, Catholic or Buddhist. If a dying human being needed me, that was all that mattered. That was the bottom line, a common denominator, a feeling all of us had out there. And to tell you the truth, Father, I never counted the costs. I really did lay my life on the line. After all, I was the Padre.

"I remember thinking, *Jesus, sweet Jesus, look, I have sinned but not all that much. Help me to get to that soldier. God, come on, don't let him die alone. God, just a few more feet!* As I jumped into his fox-hole, feelings of gratitude welled up, *O thank you God.*

Too late. He was dead.

"Despite that, I said, 'Friend, I had a hell of a time getting here to be with you, but see I did.'

"I stayed in that foxhole until the barrage was over. I wept. I prayed. And I kept on talking to the dead trooper: 'Listen friend, buddy, there was this Fella Christ who loved you very much and still does. They killed Him too. I know you must have loved Him and the things He stood for; otherwise you would not have been here to offer your own life.'

"Then I touched his forehead, rather like caressing his brow, straightening his hair, and said, 'Son, re-member me when you are in paradise.'

"I am sure he never heard me. He was dead. But somehow I know that he will do it."

When George said this, I too caressed George's jaundiced brow and said simply, sincerely, "You too,

George, remember me when you are in paradise. O.K., George?"

"O.K., Father Kaz, I will."

When George's end came, I did not have a chance to be with him, the so-called, "whiskey priest." I wanted to, I wanted to very much, but it was not to be. Neither was any other priest by his side. Somehow it was sad, very sad, that as a Catholic chaplain he had comforted, held the hand of hundreds of dying soldiers, yet he did not have a priest to be with him when he himself expired.

George, I am sure, has something much more important now: he has this "Fella" Christ by his side, holding his hand right now!

I am quite sure of that because I gave George the last sacraments a week before his death.

Priests Laugh Too

To ease pressures, to keep a sense of balance (sanity?!), most priests love a good belly-laugh. In the humor-department few will dispute that priests, as a class, overshadow every other profession, except perhaps professional comedians.

In many ways seminary life resembles that in the military. Tensions are eased by light hearted humor and banter. Pinning nicknames on each other is part of it; thus, inevitably the most brilliant student will become "Dummy" to everyone else, the bald one, "Curly," the weak one, "Horse," etc. Such nicknames will often stick with those who survive to become priests.

In the Seminary, like in any college or boarding school, there is the usual array of tricks: putting a frog or snake in another's well-made bed; sometimes itching powder or even cornflakes will do just as well. Members of the faculty are not exempt either especially those who fraternize with the students. In one Seminary, for example, the students carried a professor's Fiat into his second story class room; I know, I helped carry the car up the stairs!

Boys will be boys, and men, priests included, are still boys at heart. With the passing of years young comedians become old comedians. There are many white-haired priests with a glistening sense of humor. The same old pressures and tensions are there except in priests' lives they are real life and death situations.

So when priests get together, for deanery meetings or some relaxation, they truly enjoy each others camaraderie, relishing humorous stories, situations and jokes. There is a difference, however; their inborn or even acquired kindness through the years have taught them, by and large, to relate humorous experiences or stories about themselves, never at the expense of others, or else they will never use names.

It might go something like this: "Yes, I know the Bazurs. Know them very well. I used to pick them up for church on Sundays. I remember one time I didn't show them a very good example. It was muddy. About two miles from their house we got a flat. Changed the tire and slung it into the trunk. But wouldn't you know, three miles down the road we got another. This time we didn't have a spare, so willy-nilly I got out the inner-tube patches and the pump. The tube had at least three holes. By the time I got the tire back on I was so mad I slung the pump through what I thought was the open back window of my Model A. And BAM, there went the window too! XZ@$!"

One elderly priest who had lived alone for years in a small Saskatchewan parish was getting to be very forgetful. Still, he wanted to carry on. His parishioners loved him just as he did his parishioners. Anyway, he lived in this creaky, old rectory in which the plumbing facilities were beginning to corrode badly. One time the elbow under his bathroom sink sprang a leak.

He called the plumber who rushed in from about thirty miles away and began to work. Because of the rush the plumber had forgotten to bring a new elbow.

"Now, Father," he warned before he left, "I'll have to come in tomorrow and finish the job. So don't use the sink because there is no elbow; use the kitchen one for washing, O.K."

"Sure, son, sure."

Next morning Father gets up, puts in the rubber stopper, washes his face, and pulls the plug. Out swooshes the water on the floor! Shaking his head at his own forgetfulness, he takes the bathroom rug out to dry, and patiently mops up the floor. "Now, at last it's done," he mutters to himself as he finishes. Then, without giving it another thought, he pours the dirty water into the same sink and pulls the plug!

Once the transmission broke in his old jalopy. Instead of taking it to a garage, he figured he could save the parish a lot of money by having two high school boys fix it. After all, they always changed his tires, the oil and filter, set the carburetor and, in general, helped him get the car started in winter weather.

Taking on the job, they work all day at it. When they finish they shout to him, "Come and get it, Father, you want to try it out?"

"Sure, boys."

He gets into the car, starts the motor, shifts into reverse and, *whosh*, the car shoots ahead and knocks out the wall of the garage (only the forward gears worked but not the reverse).

As he tells of the incident later, a young priest chirps: "Well, Father, so you didn't save the parish a lot of money, but look at it this way, now you have an air-conditioned garage!"

Like any men in the U.S. Marine Corps or Green Berets, priests are not below telling salty jokes, not hard core but off-color. Such humor sheds much tension. True, perhaps because of St. Paul's injunction (Col: 3:8) some priests do not like to take part in such humor; yet they are the ones who leave the priesthood after five, ten, or twenty years.

By and large, those who tell jokes, even off-color ones (barring scandal) and enjoy hearing such, stay in the Lord's service until they die. Relieving pressure, even momentarily, and relaxing with one's comrades do help in keeping a sense of balance and proportion. A water kettle which keeps building up pressure will eventually explode.

The humor department has prevented many an explosion!

He Called Himself a Stubble-Jumper

He called himself a stubble-jumper, an image evoking barefoot boys running across the endless stubble-fields of Saskatchewan where he was born. The imagery, however, includes more than that. Prairie folk have an austere, realistic view of life, resilient and tough, but they have not forgotten how to be feeling human beings, warm-hearted and tender, always compassionate to the down-trodden. To them the runt in any litter is always the favorite, deserving extra care and affection. Strong, burly men will cry unashamedly when small children become orphaned or crippled.

People helpin' people is an unwritten principle that has never died on the prairies. Father R. imbibed this rich heritage together with the choking dust storms of summer and the bitter frosts of winter, as he did his ABCs in the one-room schoolhouse near the Alberta border.

One evening we were watching the elements in the darkening sky. The rains came down in torrents. Nature unleashing itself on the prairies is awesome, always on a grand scale. Out of the corner of my eye, I observed this grand old German priest who took his vows in 1935 in the Congregation of the Missionaries of Mary Immaculate, popularly known as the Oblates. His white hair glistening in the rain, he was in absolute glory, probably remembering many another storm in his forty two years as tenderer of Lord's flock in Saskatchewan. Just watching the torrents of rain come down, one could almost read his thoughts, *this is just what the farmers need for their grain fields at this time*. What was good for his flock was always good for him.

It was a fearful evening. To me, thunder and lightning is always like a gigantic artillery barrage at any of the main fronts in World War Two. Every few seconds the sky lights up with flashes of light and the blasts are deafening. The rains only re-enforce that feeling. I wince. Why does it always have to rain so much in wartime? Despite the warmth of summer, the rains seem cold. My body shudders at the thought of sleeping in the mud in just one army blanket.

I steal a look again at this "stubble-jumping priest" and he is beaming with smiles of understanding for his farmers. Probably recalling the lean years of the arid thirties, he muses: "Ach, Vater, this is just what the farmers need now, it has been so dry. Ya, they will have a good crop this year."

Looking up at the sky he spies an ugly, dirty gray cloud rolling about twenty, maybe forty miles away, "Vater, you know what that is. That's hail. Some poor farmers are getting it and Regina too (we are about forty miles out of Regina)."

Sure enough, after getting back to Regina, the people there tell me the ground was completely white with hail, big hail, especially in the north-west section of the city. Gardens are ruined. Some windows are knocked out. They even had a tornado warning.

A shrewd, stubble-jumper? Yes, and much, much more. His intellectual development has never stopped. Truly, the proverbial gentleman and scholar, his expertise extends far beyond the merely philosophical and theological. He can stand his own with any university professor or instructor. Being naturally curious, he has read thousands and thousands of books in the last sixty five years. He claims that he reads so much in order to keep abreast of the world about. In a way, this is surprising; in a way, it is not, because the people of the prairies have always been avid, voracious readers. Perhaps, the long, cold winter nights have something to do with it; otherwise, one can get "cabin fever" mighty early in the long, hard winter. To me at least that seems as reasonable an explanation as any. And how else explain the fact that the prairies have produced some of the greatest men and women in the history of Canada, specialists in nearly every field.

Anyway, this old stubble-jumper is God's priest down to his tip-toes. A human being, nevertheless. We all are, except that probably most of us are not quite as honest about our humaneness. His humaneness, maybe, is what makes him so understanding and compassionate about others' weaknesses and failings. In theory, his commitment to absolute truth and good is uncompromising but, in practice, his heart prevails, as it should.

He had had a difficult life. Only God and he know how difficult. Born with delicate health, he had to postpone his priestly training for three years. With boundless determination he went back to the seminary . . . and made it!

In his day, seminary training was just as tough as anything the Military can hand out in their basic training.

At any rate, he made it. And to my mind the world has been better for it ever since, because he has helped thousands of people, Catholic or not. Thousands more have been inspired by his simple sincerity, honesty, faithfulness and genuineness — and his compassionate regard of others. And they will never forget him because they became better people for having walked the same byways of life with him however momentarily.

To praise his goodness may seem like preachiness but he is the kind of person that you would want at your bedside when you are dying. And if asked he will be there, too, even if he has to drive hundreds of miles to do it. As a priest, he himself had to have three surgeries. Down to the valley of death not once but three times. Now he has only a quarter of his stomach left. Every night, like clockwork, at 3:00 A.M. his pains start which means very often no sleep for the rest of the night.

His two brothers are priests: one an Oblate missioner, and the other a Jesuit (now deceased). Two cousins are also priests. An uncle, a Jesuit priest, has survived sixteen years in a Rumanian prison or concentration camp. You might call all of them "**Fighting Soldiers From The Sky.**"

I did not know the others but they all inspired him, like he does me.

I only write about the "stubble-jumper" I know. He has tried so hard to be a good priest and he is a grand one. But after forty-two years on the spiritual frontlines, as it were, he now feels inadequate, especially with the changes in the world and its attitudes. So he has asked for a year's sabbatical or leave of absence.

Actually, he is just tired, bone-tired, after serving on God's battlefields all those years, seeing tragedy face to face. He never asked anything for himself even at the expense of his health, always serving, always being where people are suffering and hurting, where people need him. Day or night he tried to help in any way he could.

He cared for his people, cared very much. He suffered when he saw suffering in others. Now he himself is paining and needs a well-deserved rest, for things have kept eating away at him, chip by chip. Sure, many priests and ministers have experienced the same thing but they did not have the good sense to take a sabbatical or even an extended vacation until their health was completely gone.

Before his sabbatical, he pleaded, "But look, Vater, I feel so guilty. Priests are becoming fewer and fewer and I feel I am abandoning all of you, even though I need a rest."

"Hey, Father," I told him, "you are not abandoning us. Maybe if you still tried to be in the harness for another year, you would leave us for life. Maybe, by death. Maybe, by a nervous breakdown from which you might never quite recover. Either way, Father, you would never be able to help us serve the people of God anymore. But this way maybe you will still have enough health, vim and vigor, to carry on as a priest for many years.

"Hey, maybe God is trying to tell something to all of us: that we should be using our lay people more than what we have been doing. After all, there are many, many good people, stout-hearted men and women, who love God and try to help others and they are anxious to help us in every way that they can.

"Stubble-jumper, you know, I met some old North Dakotan farmers the other day. They were in Regina for a registered bull sale at the Agribition. The amazing thing was that one, a Lutheran, one a Presbyterian, the other a Methodist and I, a Catholic priest, sat down in the pool at Relax Inn and talked our hearts out. It was an honest give-and-take kind of a session.

"You know, stubble-jumper, if a person can ever feel kindness, gentleness and concern, it was in those three old North Dakotans. They cared, really cared about people like us men of the cloth. When, in one of my weaker moments, I told them that I had had it up to here (indicating a slitting motion across my throat) with my work, one of them looked at me as he would at a wounded bird and said, "Reverend, we know you have a tough job. We are one with you. Keep it up." The others extended their hand and gave me a warm handshake.

"I choked up and simply told them, "Thanks, fellas, thanks, I really need it!"

"So listen, stubble-jumper, all of us are concerned and want you to have your sabbatical for a year. Then come back to us in the land of Saskatchewan. We need you, we love you. All of us do. Never forget it, stubble-jumper!"

A Friend in Heaven

Certainly the months spent in caring for the deathly ill Dido Petro (Grandpa Peter; *dido* is a Ukrainian title of respect for any old man) made me more spiritual, I think, than dozens of retreats or parish missions that I had made in my life.

He and his wife cooked for me for about twelve years, after raising eighteen children. When she went to the Lord, he asked me if he could still continue cooking for me. He sure could and did!

He cared for my needs with such devotion and concern that I really owed it to him to care for him when he became terminally ill. He had diabetes which in the end caused gangrene in both feet. He would never complain. He was a very gentle person, never saying an unkind word about anyone.

I could not work miracles of healing like Christ but I can truthfully say I made Dido's life a little easier — giving him a little happiness in those final, painful six months of his life — lifting a glass of water to his lips, keeping him company, fluffing up his pillows, even feeding him when he was unable to feed himself. I will never forget it: he would open his mouth like a little, helpless bird does its beak for its mother to feed.

I am convinced the incidents of Christ's passion were reproduced in the last months he lived. In Gethsemane, Christ's terror was so great He sweated blood. In being sedated during his many stays in the hospital, Dido was often terrified — like the time he was convinced that they butchered him, cut out his intestines, all his insides from the neck down.

Another time during a raging blizzard outside, he said his wife and small children were dying from hunger at home and he had to go to help them. "Fadder" he pleaded, "I never asked you a favor in my whole life, but I'm asking you now, please, please take me home so that I can save them; even the cattle are freezing to death." That night cattle were freezing to death, standing up.

One time he told me, "Look at that big hole, Fadder, and that nice little pig fell into it. Please go down and take the critter out, he's so scared."

Even when he could not walk, he was convinced that the hospital attendants beat him up and chased him with sticks "way up to the front door."

When he fell in the hospital and hurt himself, cutting and bruising his forehead and opening up his hip, to him it was rats, "great big rats as big as cats who chewed me up, real deep, Fadder," he said, "see."

When being transferred to another hospital in an ambulance, he thought it was a hearse and experienced the terror of being taken to the cemetery to be buried alive. "No please, please no, not that," he begged desperately, his eyes wildly reflecting the horror he felt.

These were nightmares, not real, but to him they were very real — like Christ's terror in Gethsemane.

Christ's shame and humiliation in hanging naked on the cross was relived by Dido too. To a modest man like Dido it was always shameful to be undressed and washed by others. Even so, nothing could compare to his humiliation whenever he had a disaster in bed. Everytime it happened at home, poor Dido would silently weep like a heartbroken child. I would clean everything up, take the bedding off and his soiled clothes and wash him; then I would smile and kiss him on the forehead to assure him that it was all right, saying, "That's good it went, Dido, I'm glad because now we don't have to worry about your being plugged up anymore."

Once when this happened twice in one night, through his tears, he paid me the nicest compliment one could ever give a priest: *"Fadder, v tsilym szyrokim sviti na pevno nema tako sviaschenyka jak vy. (Father, in the whole wide world, certainly there is no other priest like you)."* No one had ever paid me a better compliment and it made all those months of caring for him so very worth-while.

Dido did not want to be a burden to anyone. Even during those weeks when the doctor forbid him to step on his feet because of the danger of gangrene spreading and we did not have a wheelchair then, I would carry him from the bed to the chesterfield or from the chesterfield to bed, but he would plead, "Father, don't carry me because you will hurt your back, I can walk myself." He would risk the gangrene turning septic because he did not want me to hurt my back. That was just like Dido. His consideration for others would show in hundreds of little ways, and always so touching — like refusing to eat supper in the hospital because the man in the next bed was not fed his supper yet!

It is sad. Dido asked so little of life, yet, during those final months in his loneliness, in his desolation, rightly or wrongly, he felt only a few cared for him enough to help him — like Christ on the cross who was forsaken by nearly everyone and felt abandoned even by His Father. Even in his sleep at home Dido would groan, and contort his face in his desolation. Then, still in his sleep he would start blessing himself, Ukrainian style, three times. I would bend over his bed and kiss his bony little hand which was so helpless now, yet which had helped so many, worked so hard to bring up his family of eighteen children. This happened night after night. Even when his mind finally went completely he just kept repeating, *"Hospody, Hospody, Hospody . . .* (Lord, Lord, Lord)."

But he is at peace now. He is in heaven, in the lovely places of paradise, with Christ whom he loved and loyally served all his life. There he can walk again. No more pain for him there, no more sorrow, desolation or helplessness. His agony is over now.

And this I know too, I personally have a real, true friend in heaven who someday will get me there too somehow — he promised me that in those months we lived his agony together. *Till then, Dido proszczaju tebe, farewell, till we meet in heaven. It was a privilege to be able to help you and I am so deeply, humbly grateful.*

Phil, A Good Guy

A good guy he was, Phil, a Viet Nam Vet, a hero no less, like so many of the 58,022 who gave their lives in that ravaged, war-torn land. To paraphrase Churchill in another context: *never have so many owed so much to so few*.

Tragic? Utterly devastating to those who gave their all and were willing to give life and limb for their country — this, despite the many people Stateside who despised and scorned them for their very sacrifice. And it happened, not once, but many times to men who endured countless fire fights far away from dear ones, with tracers firing through the night and machine gun bullets whining from dusk till dawn, any of which could have been the kiss of death. In Southeast Asia, everyone seemed to have jungle rot or pseudomonas (various bacterial infections with blue green pus). They saw buddies killed, legs blown off, faces disfigured, intestines plastered to fatigues — still so vivid as if it happened the day before. Well, to many it did happen the day before they deplaned in the U.S.A. Good ole U.S.A., they thought.

They did not expect brass bands, warm handshakes or embraces of welcome, but neither did they anticipate the stares of hatred, contempt and even spittle in their faces. Were they fighting for this? These spiteful people were not there, how could they know? They never had to land in the LZS (landing point) in the midst of fire fights; they never had to gather their best friends' hands, feet, entrails, bits and pieces of flesh, and tag them for Grave Registration points to ship back to a "grateful" U.S.A.

Their country called, conscripted them and they responded; so why did their detractors heap such scorn on them? Did they not understand how the returning GIs hurt inside. Perhaps not, because they never had to be on patrol in the green jungle hells of Nam, wading up to their arm-pits in the swamps and rivers infested with snakes and all kinds of crawling creatures. Nor were they ever at An Khe Pass ambushes or Booby Trap Alley. On the Ho Chi trail? They never had to face the RPs (types of rockets used by the V.C. or NVA) or the Bouncing Bettys.

The ones who were there so wanted their tour done so that they could come home. Come home they did — to shouts of derision and scorn. "Why are we being treated like this?" asked a Vet without a leg to the one helping him off the plane. "Did we want to be there, to be sent out on Search and Destroy Missions? To hell no less?"

Not any more than those who despised them!

Yet it had to be done. No one liked "cleaning" a village out, an "innocent" village, where only old men, women and children were found.

"V.C. here today, grandma-san?"

"No V.C."

"Yesterday, V.C. here?"

"No V.C."

"Grandpa-san, V.C. five days ago?" And the GI would hold up five fingers.

"No. No V.C."

Yet in leaving the village the company would get clobbered, sometimes with 50% casualties. Well, after the fourth such ambush, the "cruel" Americans would indeed burn down the village and raze it to the ground. Let those who would act differently cast the first stone.

Yes, small children killed too. A mere five year old comes up to the GI and pleads, GUM, GUM. As if on cue, shouting breaks out a hundred yards away. The

GI momentarily turns his head to see what is happening. Lobbing the grenade by the feet of the GI the kid disappears into the crowd and WHAM! There is little left of the GI — his entrails are hanging from a picket fence, a few feet away his jungle boot with his foot still in it and pieces of bone and flesh in a big red pool of blood. That was the GI.

Most GIs loved little kids. Perhaps because they reminded them of their own little ones left behind at Jone's Junction, Boyne Falls or Brooklyn. They liked to pick them up, to cuddle them. It happened in a bar next to the one Phil was in. The place was jammed wih GIs. A four-year old wandered in, and unbeknown to any of the Americans someone put a bomb on him and sent him into the bar. Some GI picked him up and he exploded, taking five other GIs with him.

Kids could and did kill just as surely as any black pyjama-dressed grown up V.C. did. Stateside, somehow it was the kids who got all the tears but none could be spared for the dead GIs or their families. Hate, yes. Tears, no.

The American civilians who so hated the military never wanted to know what it was like to hold the severed head of their friend in their arms, tenderly cradling it. No decent human being would ever spit on anyone who ever went through an ordeal like that, no matter what.

They should have asked any doctor, nurse, corpsman or medivac what they saw when they patched up the 303,700 Americans there in Southeast Asia. In many instances the quick and the dead were the lucky ones. The medical personnel who saw the oceans of suffering salutes with pride and honor some three million American members of the Armed Forces who served there between 1964 and 1975. After all, they did not go to Nam for a sun tan or to swim in the South

China Sea. They went to risk their lives. They fought honorably, bravely and, yes, heroically.

Some three million Americans are a lot of people, 58,022 of whom never made it back. For all that, many in the U.S.A. could care less — merely so much human refuse to be lugged in green bags to the garbage dumps.

Gratitude and welcome they got from a thankful people? Like the Marine sergeant with two and a half rows of ribbons on his chest when he landed at the Philadelphia Airport. The first words he heard were: "How did you feel killing all those innocent women and children, you murderer! How many did you kill?" Or the nurse who wheeled a quadriplegic off the plane at L.A. She knew he had a colostomy, could not have sex for the rest of his life, and therefore, he could not have kids of his own to hug. "You, bastard, you should have been killed for what you did in Viet Nam", adding insult to injury, the woman went on, "not just wounded but killed like you did the children there." The nurse later stated bitterly, "I was so angry and hurt, I cried; in fact, through the tears I couldn't see." Those were the thanks the Viet Nam Vets got from thousands of people. Why? Guilt perhaps?

The rightness or wrongness of American involvement in Viet Nam has been argued endlessly. Perhaps the higher ranks of the military were in a better position to judge its morality. Certainly the lower ranks did not; yet, what could they do? Desert? That would have been dishonorable and, in the estimation of most, wrong. They fought the dirtiest war in American history honorably and well, without deserving any hatred and insult.

Take Phil. He was just an ordinary American guy before he went to Nam. Married. Two little blond girls. He was called: He went. He was tough but did not wake his daughters to say goodbye. He did not want them to see their Daddy cry. Nor did he want his wife Corraine to go to the airport with him. When he kissed his wife Corraine, he wiped the tears from his face with his sleeve. With the sad smile he always had, he merely told her, "Honey, I'll be back again when my tour is done. I know. I am a lucky one. Take good care of Carey and Jane."

Trooper, belly in, shoulders out, marching out into the foggy night. Only once did he turn around and blow a kiss at Corraine who just stood on the doorstep silently weeping.

On the plane to Okinawa he said little; he shared his thoughts with no one, except God perhaps. Even when another grunt (infantryman) mentioned. "Good down South," (as they used to call Nam in Okinawa), he merely smiled that sad smile of his and said nothing.

When they landed in Bien Hoa, it was under rocket and mortar attack. "Come on, come on, soldier, zig zag. Next, come on, zig zag. Come on, this is no picnic, you know," the Cap. shouts. The blasts of heat gagged but they ran, ran faster than they ever did in their lives to the bunkers. Some got hit, lost their lives without firing a shot.

For Phil it was mostly OJT (on job training). For three months he was on Search and Destroy Missions: for four he was a lurp, a member of the Long Range Reconnaissance Patrol, long sweeps into the valleys of death. He was a good point man. Wounded, he was sent to Guam for a month. Then it was the DMZ and being sprayed seven times with Agent Orange.

Many things the Americans did in Nam were brutal, evil and senseless. No doubt of it. But war, any war especially Viet Nam made brutal killers out of decent men. Many never recovered emotionally, psychologically or even worse. There are still, I am sure, many many more psychologically wounded than the 303,700 physical ones. Many of the former care not whether they live or die. They still scream the names of their buddies long into the night or cry and moan in restless sleep. Do they deserve our sympathy any less than the others?

Yes, Phil was a lucky one. He thought so. His tour was done, he was alive, and going back home. When he disembarked at Frisco he wanted to kiss the ground. Despite the hate, scorn and all, he wanted to forget Nam; he figured he had a whole life to live with Corraine, with daughters Corey and Jane.

Yes, he had a whole life to live — what he did not know was that it would last only a year! CANCER. Was it Agent Orange?

I saw Phil three months before he died. He was not bitter. He smiled that sad smile of his. I spent an afternoon and evening with him. We played some poker. Drank some beer. But mostly we talked. At times he winced from the pain of the spreading cancer. At night we went to a polka party. He used to be full of life and loved polkas. As a favor he asked me to take his wife to dance a polka, for he was too weak to do it himself. I did.

Today he is buried in his village cemetery. Every week his wife visits his grave and brings flowers to put on each side of the American flag that flutters in the wind.

When years ago the troop trains with dead Americans wound their way through the countryside, some would turn away in disgust, some called them killers and worse. But these honorable soldiers are resting in peace now, in village church yards, in town graveyards, in city cemeteries. They cannot hear the taunts, the reproaches, the scorn, the shouts of hate nor the cries of derision anymore. Nor can they ever again hear the blasts of mortars, rockets or whine of the AKs (AK-47s — Soviet rifles supplied to the VC and the NVA).

But I do hope that somehow they can hear the anguished sobs of the ones who loved and appreciated them — and there were many — and it was not only wives, sweethearts, mothers, fathers, brothers and sisters, but hundreds of thousands of others. The whole of the South China Sea cannot contain all the tears from their reddened eyes.

We Salute You, Vets of Southeast Asia!

Who was Phil? Just a friend whose voice cannot be stilled from beyond the grave. Yes, just a friend.

Why Did You Take Them, Lord?

The history of accidental loss of life in the countryside (especially when one has charge of many parishes) reads like a chronicle of war. This is also true of non-Catholic parishes, I am sure. Ask any minister. Cities are not alone in having many mortalities due to accidents. The big question, however, is why Lord? Why them, not me?

Farmer John's tractor rolls over on him and he is dead within minutes. He was fifty and a father of six.

Walter falls asleep with a lit cigarette on the sofa; he asphyxiates and half his body is literally roasted before the volunteer firemen douse the fire and pull him out. He was thirty five.

Farmer Joe hits an embankment on a country-road and is DOA (dead on arrival) by the time they get him to the nearest hospital.

Another hits a freight-train in a blizzard and dies there immediately.

Joddy, age six, slips under a heavy deep tiller. It crushed him to death.

Young Mrs. Yorky dies having her first baby. She was completely under a doctor's care, yet something went wrong. A half hour before, when her husband went out for lunch she was a vibrant, expectant mother. Now she is gone. The doctor breaks the news to him. He cannot believe it.

Sam is chopping down trees. One falls on him and a bear mauls him to death. They find him the next day. He was to have his forty-sixth birthday party that evening.

Dick, Jake, Harry, Alex and Jane, four boys and a

girl, speed to a wedding and miss a curve, hitting a river bank. All are dead when they find them the next afternoon. Ages? Seventeen to twenty.

Seventy-year-old Jacob falls into a well when no one is around. His wife and sons find him when they come home from town.

Two brothers, Boris and Paul, drown in a lake, one trying to save the other. Both were in their teens and out fishing.

On a rainy Saturday night an accident involving eleven people happened right outside of town. A new highway intersected another and someone forgot to put up a stop sign. Three young men in their twenties were coming from a dance and a family of eight were returning from the movies. Two were dead; a third was disemboweled and the fourth one had a broken neck and was in a coma until death claimed her two years later. It could have been much worse.

Another time; another place. An accident involving ten. The bodies, blood and gore at the hospital were like a scene from a war movie. The nurse took me to the worst casualties: the first, a young man whose eyes were already glazing over; the second was in a coma and was not expected to survive the night; the third, a young man whose both legs were broken, as well as an arm and collar bone; no one knew how extensive were the injuries of the fourth who was found under one of the overturned cars. The rest avoided no greater injury than broken arms, or fingers.

Jerome is under a car fixing it. It falls on him and crushes him so badly that he dies in the hospital a week later.

Five of a family of six burn to death when their home is destroyed by a flash fire.

A teenager accidentally, but senselessly shot to death.

The litany can go on and on, and this does not include heart attack or death from natural causes. Death is terrible in any form but when young people die so suddenly it is an immense shock not only to the family but to all their friends and neighbors, in fact, to the whole community.

We will never answer the question of why. Perhaps God takes them when it is best for their souls. Perhaps not. I do not know. It does, however, tear the caring pastor's heart apart, despite his sincere attempts at words of comfort and consolation to others. In the meantime, everyone of us can hope that all is well with them and put the question among the first dozen to ask God when we ourselves will cross the great divide.

The Ladies Dressed in White — Nurses

We Catholics do not have a monopoly on loving Jesus. It is there for all to see in many people, in various places and climes, especially in the hospitals.

Ernest Hemingway wrote a very moving book a few years back, called *For Whom the Bell Tolls*. A nurse often hears the bell toll, that someone's end is near. Still, she controls her emotions and smilingly tries to ease the pain by making the dying patient as comfortable as possible by caressing the brow, holding the hand through the long, lonely nights. A cheery smile goes a long way. She may have been on duty for twelve hours but seems as fresh and sweet as if she had just come to work.

She speaks kind words to an old Indian grandmother who probably did not hear such benevolent words from anyone for many a year. Tears of gratitude well up in the old woman's eyes at the lady in white.

The neatly dressed, immaculately groomed old gentleman, who probably never missed showering each day for years, in the end was incontinent and soiled his bed clothes. To him that was the height of shame, utterly undignified. He never knew death is always undignified. As the lady in white cleans him up, she genuinely embraces him for his apologies and the tears that glisten in his eyes.

Those too weak to feed themselves the nurse will beg and cajole just to get a few spoonfuls of liquid food into them. Her work is waiting but this is the most important job for her now.

The Indian child who just died of leukemia. Who will break the news to its mother? Likely as not, the lady in white. She cringes not, wipes the tear from her own eye, and tries to be brave. All she can do is whisper, "I'm sorry. We did all we could. Can you believe that?" and embraces the mother by the neck and kisses her just to take away a little of that bitter sorrow.

It is the same with another mother whose two little children burned to death.

Her words are just as kind to those whose mind is gone. She jokes with them, kids them but, above all, is kind to them. That is worth a thousand words and this is telling just a part of it.

It really makes no difference whether one is Cree or Catholic, Greek or Slav, black or white. Sickness and death are the great levelers — of social, political inequalities, of all distinctions. As the Byzantine liturgy aptly puts it: "After we gain the world we then will come to live in a grave together with kings and paupers" (*Sessional Hymn - Sidalen,* Tone 6), or "Then I peered into the tombs and saw naked bones. I asked 'Who here is king, who a soldier, who a rich man or poor, who a just man, who a sinner'" (*Tones of John the Monk,* Tone 5).

As chaplain, one breezes in and out of hospitals without seeing half of it but when one is a patient himself he observes the ladies in white doing their work all day and all night long.

One day the man in the bed next to mine died. I am sure that God will place this ninety-seven year old, God-fearing Presbyterian into the mansions of the just and number him among the holy ones. His last agony lasted thirty four hours. Through his groaning, through his moaning, one could still make out his words, "Take me, Jesus. Take me, Jesus."

To me it was the most beautiful act of trust, of love that a person could make. After ninety-seven years of serving the Lord, he really could say, "Take me, Jesus," and mean it.

He died at 3:15 A.M. Tears would not come at the beauty of such trust and love. I went out into the corridor, smoked a cigarette and kept thinking of the sheer loveliness of that trust and love and decided to become a better Christian too.

A lady in white came, sat by me, patted my shoulder and quietly asked, "Father, will you be all right?"

"Certainly, nurse, "I'll even be a better Christian for it. That dear old Presbyterian taught me a lot!"

Then and there I also made up my mind never to pass by a nurse without giving her an especially nice, sincere smile . . . as a small gesture of appreciation for all the patients who should have said *thank you* and did not!

One Form of True Love

I spent three days with an old man who has lived fifty-seven years with his wife. Now she is ill, deathly sick, in a hospital. He is beside himself with worries and anxiety. He knows he has to face that ultimate truth that she will die before him.

Fifty-seven years with one person! Maybe he had not been an ideal husband in his day nor maybe even an ideal father to his children. Maybe he was, but now he knows he will be left alone, a part of him will die with her, part of him will be with her forever.

Since I got to know them, they were both kind and considerate towards one another and to their neighbors, an ideal couple. When he had surgery two years before, she was like a mother hen, fluttering about, doing all she could to ease his pain and desperation. Now that she was sick, he prayed day and night that the Lord release her from her pain and that she come home to him again.

On hearing the news, I drove two hundred miles to be with them. They were like a mother and father to me in my own time of need. With the hospital sixty miles away from their home and the restricted visiting hours, we could not spend too much time with her. At each parting they would cling to one another, offering each other comfort and a deep feeling of love and concern. To hide their true emotions, each would manage a smile and some cheery words.

Outside in the car he would sob and sob, sometimes he would get out and retch, giving full vent to the pent-up feelings in his heart.

On the way back to their home, he would talk about old times. Many days they had only milk and potatoes to eat. Both of them cleared the land with their bare hands, with her working right by his side and looking in on the baby in a wooden box near by. With their own hands, a hammer and saw, they built their first house, a log one, which sheltered them from the elements — "a nest for two goslings," he called it.

One year when the town fair took place he did not have a cent in his pocket to give to the children; there were seven of them now. She knew he liked a glass of beer and that he did not have a penny since the day they bought that second-hand hay rake. She had a dime squirreled away just for such emergencies, so she gave it to him. With a kiss, she told him, "My gentle dove, enjoy it to the fullest; you worked hard enough this summer to earn a beer. You deserve it."

"That was the tastiest beer I ever drank, Fadder, because I knew her sacrifice and the love prompting it."

Now the children were all away from home and he was alone. We said our night prayers together but then he stole out into the kitchen to pray rosary after rosary while pacing the floor. Finally, he would go to bed about three in the morning, tears still flowing unto his pillow. The rest of the night he would toss and turn. He did this for the three nights I spent with him. It reminded me of the haunting, mournful cries of a Canada goose after its mate has been killed by a hunter. The bird will circle back again and again, calling, seeking its fallen mate — waiting, pausing once in a while in its sorrowful lament for a response that will never come. It has to be the loneliest sound in the wild.

Here were two old timers who have loved each other for over half a century! Both had worked hard all their life, taking on various jobs in addition to farming, to provide for their brood of eleven healthy children. They were heroic but responsible parents. Only God knows of their efforts, will-power, hard labor and wor-ry.

Before I left, he told me: "God bless you, Fadder, for coming. Mama had cancer before, so maybe she will come home again; I hope at least for a couple of weeks."

"Dad," I said, "maybe she will and I'll try to walk you through this one."

She died without ever coming home again.

Duty, Honour, Country

The man is dying. It may be hours. It may be several days.

"Father, you don't have to kid me. I know I'm a dying man. And I would like to tell you something which I haven't told anyone, not even my wife, God rest her soul. But I feel I have to unload this off my chest for once.

"Actually, Father, the less a person knows about such things, the less he will have to suffer the rest of his life. **Duty, Honour, Country.** *This maxim is just the military's way of telling a person the things they want done. When these words are etched indelibly on his brain, he lives according to those words, rightly or wrongly. He can never completely eradicate them. They are there to stay, whether one was a tough Commando, a wily agent or a spy.*

"Duty, Honour, Country. I wish I never heard the words, Father. If one of the clandestine Forces died — and it seems most did — the National Defense Department never let the family know when, how or for what, only that it was in the line of duty.

"If you are a good agent and happen to be left alive, you yourself can never reveal to anyone what you have done: *Official Secrets Act,* you know. I suppose even now, years later (after World War II), they have their reasons, maybe even good reasons but, Father, they can stuff their *Official Secrets Act* down their %*@#. They can't do anything to me now anyway.

"Yes, Father, I have seen officers, good officers blow their brains out because they literally believed in **Duty, Honour, Country,** and in their minds they failed in their objective.

"Psychological warfare? Believe me, it exists and

not only in form of manipulating news and propaganda. Sometimes in covert operations you need teams of men to manipulate, to scheme. All sorts of things are considered. At the conference-table, all agree: 'yes, that Nazi General is good, too good, in fact, to let him live. We will have to try eliminating him to avoid defeat in this sector. By all means, he has to die. The quicker, the better. Scheme, manipulate, make it look like his own government found him unacceptable, a traitor no less; try to make it look as if his own people were glad he decided to commit suicide. All of you know his brilliance. That is why he has to die. Go to it now and good luck.' So you may succeed. If you do, you are wretchedly unhappy, unless, indeed, you are a killer by instinct. If you do not succeed, you are equally wretched because you have failed in your objective.

"In the 'field,' you have to kill over and over again; sometimes silently with a knife or a piece of wire; sometimes with your bare hands; only rarely with a bullet. For weeks and years you have nightmares. Even in your dreams you use every trick in the book to win; you use your feet, karate chops, the works. You wake up breathing heavily and sweating. You are not really protecting yourself but your mission. You are protecting **Duty, Honour, Country:** that is the all-important thing, not your life.

"I personally always felt sorry for the young women and girls we had to use. One young lady — never did know her real name for only cover names were ever used because if the Gestapo cracked the agent's true identity, it was curtains — died at Ravensbrück. But before that, she was a very valuable agent. Nerves of steel. One day the Gestapo were inspecting the train thoroughly, compartment by compartment, opening all suitcases. Her suitcase happened to contain a wireless transmitter. Asked what was in there, smiling sweetly she answered in her impeccable German, 'Why don't you know, a wireless transmitter, of course.' *'Danke schön, gnädiges Fraulein'* ('thank you, kind Miss') and they did not even bother to open it!

"A close shave, if you know what I mean. It probably never happened again to anyone else in the whole war.

"In front of evil a person's whole body shakes, especially when facing the Gestapo! The very word sent shivers up and down one's spine. At least it did mine. Evil men, very evil. Yet so many young men and women volunteered to jump into enemy territory. Most were dead before the war ended. They knew that it would be so. They knew that but they volunteered. **Duty, Honour, Country.** They may have died without knowing that we really cared about them, really cared, but we did. It was like losing good friends, one by one. Well, they were our friends, dear friends.

"France, 1943. Clare. I always wondered how she died. Captured? I think not, her spirit was to die, to die fighting. She was braver than I ever was.

"France, 1944. Julie. We heard she died at Oranienburg. She probably never knew that it was my decision which sent her out into the night sky, to that little town in central France — by that time I was back in England training others. Thirty years later I still think of her and wonder how she died. Was she tortured terribly before she breathed her last? She was captured at the drop before she could do anything. But that was all right; she was willing to suffer anything for **Duty, Honour, Country.**

"Jean-Paul, Tambour, Jacques, Tess, Brig and the rest. I sent all of them out there to die. We would say, *"Bonne chance, mes Amis, adieu (Good luck, my friends, Good-by), or usually, "Àbientôt' (See you*

109

soon). With me this time it will not be *'Àbientôt'* but *'pour éternite'* . . .

"Now, Father, I'm tired, very tired. I just want to sleep."

He is still sleeping, buried in his ancestral town somewhere in Quebec.

Threshing the Old, Nostalgic Way

Many people still remember the way they used to thresh. It was the highlight of the year on the farm. I saw it a couple of times when I first came to Saskatchewan.

The farmer cut the grain with a binder, then stooked it to dry. When dry enough many farmers hauled it into stacks so that they would not need as many teams and wagons when threshing time came.

In preparing for the threshing, a farmer butchered a young steer to have plenty of meat on hand to feed the working crew. Most of the time, unless the farm was small, a pig was not enough. Eggs and hens made up the difference if needed. The hard-working men were hearty eaters. Barring rainy-days and break-downs, however, the housewife had enough provisions to last a few extra days anyway.

Most outfits stayed a week or two. Lucky the farmer who finished without break-downs or rainy-days. This could hold up the threshing for days, yet the farmer had to feed the whole crew, twenty or thirty men. Most of the neighboring ladies would also come to help in preparing the food (expecting the same service in return when the threshers came to their home). The rivalry between the women in the matter of providing and preparing the food was friendly but serious. Every woman wanted "her" home the best place to eat.

When the threshers came with their huge machines, neighbors, relatives and friends came to help (again, always expecting the same favor in return). Awesome steam engines or later huge tractors pulled the equally awesome thresher, called the separator. All the youngsters loved to watch the strange machines.

When the outfit finished one farm, it would move on to the next and so forth. Most of the threshing began after freeze up, for the fall plowing and other sundry tasks had to be done before winter set in.

The evening before, a table, the size of the largest room, was set up for breakfast. The tablecloth was spread, cream pitchers and sugar bowls were set at strategic intervals and usually a cruet with at least five compartments for pepper, salt, oil, vinegar and mustard was placed in the middle of the table. They boiled the potatoes, sliced the bacon and readied a pot of eggs for boiling in the morning. Boiled eggs were easier to get ready than fried ones anyway. In the early morning all the ladies would have to do was to fry the bacon and boil the eggs, slice a couple of loaves of bread, warm the baking powder biscuits and put the butter and pitchers of syrup on the table.

During the day the crew drank gallons and gallons of water. At noon it was usually meat, potatoes and other vegetables: for desert it would be rice pudding with raisins and cream or else pies or cake. Served at the end of the day's work was supper with little variation of menu from dinner.

In setting up for the job, the threshers would park at one of the stacks and line up the machines so that the long belt, driving the separator, would not keep falling off. That done, the pitchers climbed up the stack to the highest part of the separator. After the signal to start was given the threshers threw down the sheaves to the platform or "table". There two binder-twine cutters cut the bands with knives and threw the rest, the unthreshed grain, into the feeder (later models chopped the twine with the straw). When the great belt gathered enough speed, the sound was rhythmic but soon it became a roar. The straw itself was blown out at the back into a pile and moved aside when necessary. This was done either by men with pitch forks or with "straw horses." Men carried the sacks of grain from the threshing machine to the granaries literally on their backs. When everything was going right, the hum of activity could be heard yards and yards away.

During the threshing, the crew kept no fixed hours. Most of the time it was dawn till dusk. The fireman responsible for the boiler would get up at three in the morning in order to oil the machines, get up enough steam and, in general, get everything readied for an early start.

Despite their gruelling labor, after work the men would sing, have a bit of fun by arm wrestling, broad jumping, wrestling, high jumping and certainly playing practical jokes on one another, many of which were naughty enough not to mention here. The work was hard and long but the men managed to entertain themselves after dark. On Saturday nights the crew went into town for drinks and entertainment. They were mischievous but good willed.

The "good old days" were really not as good as some of the old timers will make them out to be — probably due mostly to nostalgia. Happy times, yes; prosperous times, no. After the farmer paid his bills for the binder-twine, feeding the men and horses, and payment made to the owner of the threshing outfit and for any machinery bought during the year, the farmer had little left from his crop for his long hours of toil.

Times changed and with it came progress. With more and more farmers buying combines, less and less of them needed to hire threshing machines.

In musing about the "good old days" many an old

timer, with a sad, nostalgic smile, leaves the distinct impression that the old way of threshing was the best. It was not. It is the difference between cruising down the freeway in a sleek, new Caddie and driving a horse-drawn buggy down a country road.

Ah yes, Sport, but all the romanticism has gone out of prairie living! The price of progress, Gramps, the price of progress!

Fools and Blizzards

A fool steps where angels fear to tread — but what angel would want to tread in a blizzard anyway? God, however, must have a great fondness for fools, for I am no angel and somehow He took care of me for twenty two years out in the north country. Winter after winter it was the same, miles and miles of travel, sometimes through forests where no one lived.

The storm probably will not be a bad one, I would figure, so without another thought in the world, I would jump into the car and drive off. If God had hair, He probably tore them out long ago.

Time and time again the radio announcer would warn, in doomsday tones, of an approaching blizzard. The following day, of course, would dawn bright and clear with nary a breeze to stir the hoarfrost from one's mustache. A person gets to live with such "slight" miscalculations in weather forecasting on the prairies. To put it another way, let us say hardly anyone believes them much any more.

Of course, they all insist on a person stashing a survival kit in the car — in case one gets stuck it will save one from freezing to death until the storm abates or someone comes to help. In a pinch even several candles will do the trick. From the hundreds of candles in church I always kept forgetting to put a few into the glove-compartment of the car. How can a person be expected to remember such mundane things on fine, sunny days? No candles, no help from them — in emergencies. Several times I did buy some candy bars (to stem my hunger in case of being marooned for three or four days; they will keep body and soul together for that length of time). These, however, were usually consumed long before an intelligent cat can say *ouch*— for snacks on long drives between mission churches. Is it my fault that I am blessed with a sweet tooth?

The canned heat? I never knew anything about that; hence, never got any. You see I am naturally shy about asking store-keepers where anything is stored, even if it means going without. Besides, it saved some money too.

In emergencies, too, a person is supposed to put plastic next to the skin, under the underwear, to keep one's bodily heat in; well, I did have a garbage bag but only about half of me could get into that! Moreover, who wants to strip naked in forty-five below zero weather? Freezing to death is less of an agony in my books.

Always in a rush, especially when late for services or sick calls, never to this day did I think about bringing an extra parka or a blanket. Guess God is, indeed, fond of fools but several times He did test me but good, in fact, quite severely. Oh I prayed very sincerely, "Lord, if You get me out of this one, I'll be the best priest in town" — that was easy to keep; I was the only priest for miles around, so it was a safe bet! "And, Lord," I continued, "as soon as I hit town, if You help me make it, I'm getting that survival kit together this time for sure and put it in the car right away, no matter how rushed I am. Honest, I will, Lord." It was not to be, however. Somehow I always managed to get railroaded every time, even when I was actually on my way to the three general stores "downtown." Nothing really important: coffee with friends in the cafe, talking with a little old lady parishioner, a teacher who wants advice on how to handle a difficult pupil and, before the cows came home, the village lights went on and the stores closed. And that was that.

A person can get acclimatized to cold temperatures

116

when exposed to cold (not frigid) weather over and over again. Maybe the scientists can explain the technicalities. Actually, a person can endure the cold for hours provided he follows a few simple rules: never face the wind; being exposed, the nose, cheeks, and chin can easily get frostbitten; tears will flow, the eyes get bruised and half blinded. Body heat can also help. To warm the hands, one should put them under the armpits; that will warm them a bit. The face and nose should often be checked for frostbite. At the beginning of frostbite the skin gets white. To treat frostbite one of the worst things a person can do is to rub the frozen skin with snow. Massage is no better if one wishes to avoid permanent injury. The best way is rapid rewarming in warm water (about 104 degrees).

The north wind of the Cree is called *Keewatin*. Usually there is a calm before the storm, literally, a stillness which one can feel. Even the animals, ever sensitive, with magnificently primitive instincts become utterly still. It is as if all life has vanished. The storm comes in stealth and brings with it the big cold. The *Keewatin* blizzard may blow for three, four or five days without let up. The blizzard is fierce with no East, West, North or South. Sometimes one cannot see ten paces ahead.

When stuck in a blizzard, stay with the car. Do not panic; sooner or later help will come. Even for calls of nature, never go beyond the sight of the car; this alone may be lifesaving. A person can very easily get disoriented in a fierce blizzard, about as fast as a pilot of a piper cub in gigantic cumulus clouds.

When the *Keewatin* finally slackens and blows itself out, all is white, a totally white world, with mounds and mounds of snow which obliterate the familiar ground and landmarks. The whole world seems a huge deepfreeze.

If the people of Yakutsk (Siberia) can endure their winters, one of the coldest and longest on earth, I am sure the people of Canada can too. The housewives in Yakutsk buy their milk in icy blocks and their men drink 190 proof vodka in wintertime (available, by the way, *only* in Siberia) because normal vodka freezes there in winter. Perhaps this is a Russian touch which can teach us Canadians a little about human anti-freeze.

Human antifreeze or not, I got stuck in one of the fiercest blizzards Canada can offer. Fun? Not on your life boy! Longjohns, heavy trousers, sweater, gloves, and a leather ski-cap with a scarf wrapped around my head over the cap, as additional cover for my ears, did not seem much protection. I still felt the wind as if in a wind tunnel. Foolishly, I spent ten precious minutes shovelling. I should have paid more attention the previous night to the ring around the moon which, I swear, in winter presages snow.

Fortunately, I saw a light flickering ever so dimly about a half a mile away. Even so, when I got to the farmhouse, my ear lobes were frozen like pieces of bacon. I could break them off by bending them sharply. I did not try though — they go nicely with the face. For five years, however, they would open up and some liquid (whatever it was) would ooze out.

That flickering light from the farmhouse saved me though. A friend of mine froze to death only several yards from his own house. He just wandered around in circles without recognizing his own farmyard. But it is like that in a fierce blizzard.

When I get into town, Lord, into the trunk goes that survival kit. This time for sure!

Three days later the roads were open but no survival kit went into the car. In all honesty, though, it was not entirely my fault. A family was waiting for me in order to make funeral arrangements for their mother. That done, time permitted me only to change my clothes and rush to the church for Sunday Mass. The sermon I kinda made up on the way.

A funny thing happened during the sermons (bilingual: Ukrainian and English). In my hurry I had forgotten to fasten my belt securely. As I was waxing strongly in the sermons, I felt my trousers slipping down ever so gradually — lower and lower! To stem the downward trend (it just would not do to have a man of God's pants come down during a sermon), in panic, I spread my legs further apart. But it was still a losing battle. So out went the legs further and further apart until I was absolutely spread-eagle. Whatever my parishioners thought of my stance, they surely could not have heard shorter sermons than those!

The Tuesday of the funeral was crystal-clear but the thermometer stood at fifty-six degrees below zero Fahrenheit. This time I was determined to beat the cold: two pair of underwear under woolen trousers, thick sweater, heavy overcoat and fur cap — the works. Only one thing went wrong: as I bent over to mark (the Ukrainians call it "sealing") the grave, I could hear a loud rip (probably half the mourners must have too). I finished the funeral bravely but wisely declined to take off my overcoat for the traditional dinner afterwards.

Lucky I did, too. Later in the privacy of my rectory I examined the damage: not only was one of the underwears ripped but the whole backside of the trousers was too. Well, it was something to write back home to Michigan about.

Yes, God looks after fools in more ways than just in blizzards and cold I guess.

A Hunter I Am Not

A hunter or a fisherman I am not. I hate to kill anything anymore. To fishermen I always said, "How would *you* like to be dragged across the pool with a great big hook in *your* mouth?" Moose and elk scare me. Deer less so, but, they are too nice to kill. It is like shooting Bambi! Picking mushrooms and berries is more my style.

A Jewish friend, Sal, who owned a motel in Northern Michigan, kept writing me to say how he would like to come for a visit and shoot some Canada geese.

So one day Sal drove up, bringing his motor home, two shotguns (one for himself, the other for me) and a young registered black Labrador retriever. Truly, a beautiful animal. Was he ever proud of that dog! To hear Sal talk, one would think all the dog would not do was to pluck and roast the birds.

After showing Sal the local sights, whatever there were of them, we took off for the goose country.

During the trip I learned quite a few new English words, four letter ones — and a few Yiddish ones too! Though a main highway, the road had quite a few potholes: some, I swear, a foot deep. Saskatchewan's main highways today are absolutely superb, compared to what they used to be. Every time we hit a pothole at sixty miles per hour, Sal would let out a string of expletives that Webster's Unabridged Dictionary is ashamed to carry. "Slow down, Sal, slow down. We'll get there and the geese will still be there. Their winter vacation in Texas begins next month!" But a mile down the road the process would be repeated, and repeated — and repeated.

There was no motel in Goosetown and the hotel was full, so five miles out of town we found accommodations with a charming, elderly German couple. It was too cold to sleep in Sal's motor home.

Next morning we dug the pit, camouflaged it, and put out the decoys. He gave me a shot gun and a box of shells (knowing I needed ten boxes to bring down a goose). His instructions were simple: "When they come over, just jump out of the blind and shoot in their general direction."

When the geese came swooping in, I stood up, took general aim, as per instructions, and *bam*. The gun kicked, of course, and walloped me in the jaw, a wallop that made me spin and reel. He laughed so hard, he did not get a goose that time either (which made me secretly, fiendishly gloat).

Before the evening was over, he bagged ten. I bagged none, though the jaw stayed sore for three days. All in all, during our stay, he got thirty-six geese and I expended three boxes of shells but did get one goose for my efforts. No one was near me that time, so I really did get one — though I shot at the first one in the V, the fifth fell out of the ranks.

One day it began drizzling, so we decided to shoot some ducks. He got a duck on his first shot, though it fell into the drink (water). Here was Sal's chance to prove how good a retriever his black Lab was. The dog ran to the edge of the water, put his front paw into it, shivered and scampered back to his master! This time it was my turn to laugh. It really was funny. I snickered and chuckled till we got back to the house. In fact, my laughter was well-nigh uncontrollable — without inhaling any laughing gas either! The dog never did go into the water all that season; not that I blame him, for the water *was* cold.

Another rainy day. More duck shooting. We knew exactly what field was best, for we "spotted" it the evening before. We got up at dawn, put out the decoys, and crawled under the swaths (windrows of cut wheat, oats or barley) though they were quite wet and cold. Huge flocks of ducks came swooping down, alighting on the windrows; in fact, soon the swaths were black with them. Sal shot first from a semi-prone position straight down his windrow. Ten ducks in one shot, which is about the best any hunter can do. Delightedly, he gathered them into a burlap sack to show off his prowess in town — even I shot a duck that time.

No more hunting that day for he was determined to show off his hunting prowess as soon as possible. We arrived in town, as if for breakfast. As luck would have it, there were about ten men standing by the cafe. He took the burlap bag off the truck and proudly proclaimed, "See, fellas, ten with only one shot", and promptly dumped the birds unto the sidewalk. It is hard to believe but five of the ducks had been merely stunned: these simply picked themselves up and flew away!

For a moment Sal stood there aghast, mouth open, utterly incredulous and venting Yiddish expletives even I did not hear on the potholed roads. Everyone else, however, was in stitches.

It was with good reason that someone long ago came up with the adage: **One Bird in the Hand is Worth Two in the Bush.**

How true! How true!

A Doukhobor or Secret Catholic?

The Doukhobors are Russian "spirit wrestlers," no more or no less, a good people from Trans-Caucasia, brought into Western Canada by Leo Tolstoy and the English Quakers. They first came in 1899 and soon 7,500 settled in three colonies of Saskatchewan, two north of Yorkton and one southwest of Prince Albert.

They held their property in common, were self-sufficient, good farmers, hardworking and thrifty.

Most people remember the Doukhobors from the old days when they marched "looking for Jesus." On one march in which a considerable number of them took part, they walked barefoot on the snow-clad ground to Yorkton and wanted to go further. When asked where their boots were, one of them replied, "Jesus boots," and raised one of his bare feet off the ground to show that his feet were God-given.

The more fanatical minority, later known as the Sons of Freedom, would strip, and march naked, utterly naked, to protest government interference and in search for freedom.

They believed the words of Christ that no one should be too overly attached to earthly things. So they believed. It took a lot of believing. Honestly, how many of us have that type of deep faith.

So many people only remember the Doukhobors' stripping of garments. Being curious and prurient enough to cluck their disapproval, they rushed out to see them naked, but the faith of the Doukhobors was much more than that.

Ask any of my Ukrainian old-timers, many of whom the Doukhobors helped. When the CNR dumped the Ukrainians in the bushland which was then the Yorkton district on the Western prairies of Canada, some of them did not have a dime to their name and no prospects of any in a long time to come. Men wept as they saw wife and children hungry, crying in the middle of nowhere and weary, bone-weary with every step to get to relatives or their fellow-villagers in Norquay, Fort Pelly, Arran or Swan Plain.

Just as they had no idea exactly where they were going, so they had no idea just how huge the country was, how endless the prairies were. They went through scrub-forests and more forests. They stumbled on, hoping in the right direction. It was unreal! After all, the CNR agents in the Ukraine told them if they came to Canada, the government would give them more land for free than their *Pan* (nobleman, landowner) had in the old country. "It's all there, for you," they said, "just for coming and claiming it." They believed. They came. Now all this. Nobody cared. Nobody listened and those who did, did not understand their language. Still they came in droves from the Western Ukraine.

Many passed through the Doukhobor *Selenia*, communal villages. They were never turned away. Years later the old timers told me, "At least here we understood much of what was said. *Nekrescheny Doukhobory*, the unbaptised Doukhobors. Nobody told us about them in the old country. At first we thought they were Orthodox Russians about whom we had been warned. Our priests had told us about them, that they wanted to take over our souls, to bring us into their fold. Yet, here were these people speaking Russian but claiming to be Doukhobors, not Orthodox. Doukhobors? We never heard of them, still they were a decent, kind people. And we were grateful."

126

As soon as the Doukhobors would see strangers coming, they would rush out to greet them in the name of Christ: "*Da*, you probably did not eat for a long time, let us give you something to eat." They did not have much but they would give the Ukrainians borsch, potatoes and cabbages. Their religious beliefs forbade them to kill animals: "it is forbidden to kill an animal." And they were strict about it: no slaughter of animals even for food.

They would not butcher animals but they would give the strangers, my Ukrainians, a calf, a cow or vegetables to hold them over the winter, "so that they would not want." They believed in Christ, His teaching, His way, as they understood it. No ifs or buts.

They also refused to bear arms; this got them into trouble with the Tsarist government. That is why they moved to Canada — to live in peace with their fellow men.

Unbaptised Doukhobors! But to their credit, they helped many in getting settled in Northeastern Saskatchewan when there were no welfare agencies, no unemployment offices. The Canadian government at the time did not seem to care whether the Ukrainians and other Slavs lived or died in this new land, but the Doukhobors did.

They detected in the Slav peoples one of their own brothers in a vague kind of way. They felt it. "You are one of ours," they would say. Maybe they would have helped any human being. I suspect that they would.

Yes, they gave all they had. Maybe it was because they themselves went through hell and back — if we may use the expression — when they first came to Saskatchewan. These were the years when all the men went out to acquire cash by working for earlier settlers, and the women literally put on harnesses to plow the fields and till the land themselves because at the time they had no oxen or horses with which to do it. Yes, ten or sixteen would harness themselves to the plow. And from that labor they found it within their hearts to share with the less fortunate.

God bless all the Doukhobors. I have attended their marriages-weddings; I have gone to their funeral services and listened to their plaintive chants and, in a sense, they have inspired me, a Catholic priest, to say my own prayers as sincerely as possible, especially the public ones. Listening to their prayers and how piously they prayed, I understand now a little bit better why their forefathers broke with the established Church of Russia and the *popy* (priests) who used to recite their prayers by rote, mechanistically, like Buddhist prayer wheels.

Yes, they say the Doukhobors slept in communal bedrooms, husband, wife, beside their children. They say sometimes things kinda got mixed up, a husband going to another man's wife, or a wife to another man. That I do not know, but I do know that they loved Christ maybe more than I, a kinda straight-laced priest.

Well anyway, when I was stationed in Regina, the Latin Rite chaplain phoned from the Plains Health Centre for me to administer the sacraments to this elderly gentleman, a Mr. Smirnoff, who was about to go to the Lord with terminal cancer. The chaplain told me Mr. Smirnoff was a Ukrainian Catholic and did not know English, so I rushed to his sick bed without giving it much thought, introduced myself and asked him where he was from. Buchanan, Saskatchewan. I asked him if he used to know people by the name of Chicilo, Brzezinski, Hrynchyshyn, Yasinski and a few others. His face lit up with pleasure at the thought of them. They used to be neighbors, all of them.

After hearing his confession by question and answer, I tell him I bring Christ in Holy Communion. In receiving Chirst he cries and I cry. Both of us pray together for a while and I give him the last Anointing of the Sick, knowing that his hours are limited. Hundreds of times I have had the feeling, *Dear brother of mine, the next time I see you it will be in paradise.*

Only after I drive out of the hospital parking lot did the thought strike me out of the blue: *his name is Smirnoff! God, did I give the sacraments to a Doukhobor?* Later, I asked a parishioner, who used to work around Buchanan. Was Smirnoff a Catholic or Doukhobor?" Sure enough, he was Doukhobor!

Well, I tell myself, he must have been worthy, he received Christ with all the affection and love he could muster. Christ came to him in those last hours and, I am sure, walked him hand in hand through the valley of death. Smirnoff died the next day. His face peacefully content and radiant.

The Touch of God

Anyone who truly loves people can often unlock the innermost recesses of their souls. Such a person will soon get to know of the endless, aching need of the divine felt by every human heart . . . and how each responds, each in its own way, according to its faith.

God's ways are mysterious indeed. Grace, the ever tender touch of God on the soul comes in many forms and, when needed, it is never found wanting. Sometimes it is found under stooped shoulders, sometimes beyond the tears and sobs. At other times it caresses the soul with the sheer joy and rapture of being alive. Always present, it forever pursues, is ever solicitous and caring. Its presence can be seen, it is true, in the glistening eyes of an up-turned face, in the out-stretched hands, in the bended knees, the bowed head, but more importantly the touch of God shows itself in the quiet dignity and sheer heroism of those faced with soul-wrenching pain, misunderstanding, heartbreak and, most difficult of all, death itself.

Sandy was a lively, fun-loving beauty of twenty-three. Her beauty was breath-taking by any standard. Her loveliness would make the heart of an eighty year old man exult but her comeliness never made her vain. Her hunger for God showed itself in her rapt attention to the word of God as she sat beside her mother every Sunday in church.

Young as she was, Sandy was an executive in one of the government departments in Regina. One day she came home and told her mother that something must have happened to her hand, that she could not hold a pen. After extensive medical testing, including a cat-scan, the verdict was clear and deadly: an inoperable brain tumor; three months of life at most was all they could say.

Yes, she was terrified but brave, very brave. Perhaps she had received her bravery from her mother Miriam. Years back, as a school teacher, her mother used to drive twelve miles of country roads, sometimes through blizzards, sleet, and storm to earn enough to feed her brood of four after the death of her young husband. In an unguarded moment she told me how she used to pray in especially fierce blizzards that God spare her life, to bring her safely back home to her babies. One of her sons died at the age of ten, a daughter at six. Now she only had Sandy and a retarded son. "Father, I never asked God for much, only for strength, but now I feel I have so little of it left. Father, please pray for me."

They tried cobalt treatments, massive doses of radiation, and finally chemotherapy to prolong her life. Her face became bloated, its complexion pallid. Her hair, her beautiful raven hair fell out. Only her inner beauty shone through in a quiet, calm way. Whatever she was thinking, whatever she was suffering she successfully concealed behind her wane smile. No matter. I always had a lump in my throat whenever I brought her Christ in Holy Communion. In the solemn hush, I would whisper, "Kid, put in a good word to Christ for me too." Invariably, she would answer, "You know I will, Father. Try to see Mother. She seems so dejected."

When she was well, Sandy used to love attending concerts of the Regina Symphony. She donated a lot of her time working at the *Centre of the Arts* just to be able to hear the great artists of our time. Her record collection included the world's best. In between hospital bouts she would sit for hours listening to Mozart, Haydn, and Tchaikovsky on her stereo.

Only once did her fierce determination, her indomitable courage fail. One afternoon Sandy was sitting on the sofa listening to Nana Mouskouri's rendition of the *White Rose of Athens*, one of her favorites. Her mother tiptoed into the room to share the mood of the moment with her . . . tears were silently streaming down Sandy's face. Without quite knowing what to say in comfort, her mother sat down beside her and simply took her hand into hers. All of a sudden Sandy's silence gave way to loud, wrenching sobs and a desperate cry for help, "I want to live, Mother, I so want to live . . ."

She quickly climbed out of her valley of tears, never to re-enter it again. Wiping her face with the back of her hand, she whispered, "Forgive me for my moment of weakness, Mother, I know life is even tougher for you. It's all in the hands of God." With a kiss, she added, "Mother, I'm something like that white rose . . . could you put a white rose on my casket . . ."

"Of course, darling, of course."

Sandy was a fighter, a great conquering spirit. She never hoped for a miracle. She was too much of a realist for that but in facing death she was never defeated. In the final months she willed herself to accept her intense suffering without flinching, without wincing. The touch of God on her soul was there for all to see.

I had the funeral. For the eulogy I merely explained why, amid the clouds of incense and the flickering candles, there were no flowers except the white rose on her casket. It was sad, yet somehow deeply consoling for everyone knew why she wanted it that way.

Till the white rose blooms again . . . Sandy. *Goodby, goodby till then.*

Loneliness On the Prairies

Loneliness, lonesomeness, is about the most painful word in the English language. Certainly some suffer from it more often than others. Some suffer it rarely; others, almost every day. The great distances, the lack of contact with others, solitude and desolation are especially evident on the prairies. That is why many call them the *lonely prairies*.

Loneliness is truly another way of saying: **Wanted — A Friend**. No more, no less. It cannot be avoided nor evaded. In a sense, it is incurable. Sensitive people and priests are particularly prone to it, but it can afflict anyone, the farmer on the tractor, a housewife alone all day in her kitchen, a child without brothers, sisters or close friends at school or church. Another way of putting it: loneliness is naked sadness.

Wanted — A Friend is an expression of a heart yearning to love and cherish someone with whom a person dares to be oneself, to be able to bare his naked soul. A friend only wants his friend to be what he really is, neither better nor worse. He understands that one can really open up to a friend. He knows, sees and loves the person just for what he is. Yet many people seem to have no one to share it all with them. We know that the human heart, of course, is meant to love God and will find no rest until it finds itself with Him, but that does not rule out human friends and affection.

Distances on the prairies are great. Contacts relatively few. Aristotle once put it wisely, "Many a friendship is lost through lack of speaking." Due to the distances involved contacts among the prairie people are few; so there is a lack of speaking and we may amend Aristotle by saying that friendships here are not lost but that deep friendships cannot easily be formed. Loneliness begets depression. Perhaps that is why in the pioneering days many housewives became alcoholics. They tried to drown their lonesomeness in the bottle.

Pious platitudes, slogans of faith, avail nothing; these are mouthed by people, especially by puppets in glamorous robes who wave their arms in the pulpit. They preach what they never experienced, what they never felt: "Christ is near, He is your friend, speak to Him!" While this may be true and a panacea for some saints perhaps, it does not help many, believe me. Perhaps restless minds, brilliant ones, will never understand loneliness and depression.

True, there is God: Francis Thompson aptly compares Him to the Hound of Heaven as tirelessly pursuing and relentlessly calling an individual heart. People believe that but, being delicate creations with emotions and a nervous system, which can stand only so much, they still yearn for a deep friend on earth to whom they can show affection, touch, see and converse honestly and truly with that person. They need a friend. That is the long and short of it!

This holds true for most people; yet for one reason or another, some do not have a deep, true friend in the whole world. There are others "out there" just as lonely and desolate but which ones? Where? There may be thousands even millions of people around, probably persons just as lonesome. There is a lot of truth to the saying *Lonesome as a hillbilly in New York City*. Many people try to hide their loneliness with gaiety, laughter and cheerfulness, but that is only a shell. Such persons want to hide their true self, a self that can be more true, gentle, kind and beautiful than any storybook romance can ever describe. A casual attempt to "sweep one off his feet" is only asking for hurt and more desolation.

Even worse is a betrayal by a person whom one considered to be a true friend. Perhaps of all the pains of heart which Christ suffered was the betrayal of Judas Iscariot, whom Jesus trusted and loved. From among all human faults a person finds betrayal by a friend hardest to forgive.

Wanted — A Friend. Of all the callings the loneliest is that of priests. At least our non-Catholic confreres have wives. Each of them knows he has someone to love him, care for him, be deeply concerned and solicitous about him. Marriage has its own burdens, it is true, but the good outweighs the bad. In addition, our married, non-Catholic confreres have someone who also provides companionship, does the cooking, cleaning and laundering.

Some of the loneliest people on earth I met were unmarried priests. I still feel the moisture in my eyes when I think of them. Yes, their people love them but generally in a superficial way, no one to call their own. And when the chips are down the parishioners are concerned, as they should be, with their own families and problems. For better or for worse the priests stand alone, desolate and forsaken. It is amazing that the scandals of bottle and women are so relatively few among priests. In their loneliness some literally wept. They were good priests; maybe loneliness is what makes them so sympathetic and understanding to others, to sinners.

Living alone, some develop interesting hobbies. Others go golfing, fishing and hunting. Under the circumstances, all this is good, certainly better therapy than nervous breakdowns, strait jackets or climbing walls. Simply and honestly, priests do not crave

137

sympathy, only understanding that they, too, are human beings; that they, too, have the same feelings and emotions as everyone else. They have chosen to stay unmarried as sacrifice to God, the best they could have offered. Most have never regretted their choice. They made a decision. They stuck by it.

It is true, they may not have thought of everything when they originally made that decision but, in general, they knew what most of it entailed. It was like that with the prophet Jeremiah who lived during the sixth-seventh century before Christ. Leading a contented, peaceful life, he was reluctant to answer God's call. But God told him: "Before I formed you in the womb I knew you; before you came to birth I consecrated you; I have appointed you as prophet to the nations." (Jr. 1:5).

After alibis and excuses why he should not become a prophet, Jeremiah finally relented and answered God's call. He became a prophet, and a good one, too. As prophet, he felt lonely, rejected and suffered as all who bear witness to God's message and have to deal with people. He was misunderstood and misquoted: "Yes, even his own brothers and family played him false," as the Old Testament reveals (Jr. 11:12). It made Jeremiah cry to the Lord that the Lord fooled him and he let himself be duped.

Maybe there are days when every priest, even good ones, feel that way: that he has been duped by God. He wonders why he ever became a priest, particularly on days when he feels inadequate, incapable, that his preaching is ineffective, that he cannot please everyone.

By far and large, however, nearly every priest, in spite of his loneliness and the occasional feeling of WANTED — A FRIEND, would not trade his calling for anything else in the whole world.

How Does a Priest Think?

In the parishes, priests meet tragedy face-to-face far more often than most people think. In the countryside tragedies happen less often than in the cities. Country pastors, therefore, get more time to recover from such soul-wrenching experiences. City pastors, on the other hand, may face the victims of car accidents, heart attacks, home-disputes, of rape, of shootings on almost daily basis, especially if they have a huge hospital within their parish boundaries.

Regina has three huge hospitals: the *General, Pasqua* and *Plains.* To these, ambulances bring the seriously ill not only from the city itself but from the outlying areas of about half the province where the small hospitals do not have the sophisticated equipment to keep the critically ill alive in many cases. The two overworked pastors of St. Basil's parish and of St. Athanasius must also take care of the spiritual needs of all Ukrainian Catholics in those three hospitals.

When they often see tragedy first-hand, with real people in real life then, much of the churchy talk and controversy going on throughout our Ukrainian Catholic Church today leave them cold and wondering why many people and church leaders have nothing better to do than argue about calendars (Julian or Gregorian), the proposed patriarchate or whether the liturgical services should be in Ukrainian or English. Why cannot, they wonder, such people be more concerned about the real needs of our people and Church, the critical need for good priests, for example.

Priests are becoming fewer and fewer and, if our Church does not have priests, good priests, then the frenzy about calendars, language and the patriarchate is all for naught anyway.

How many times, for example, have priests stood, as I have, at the bedside of a young mother of four and watched her die; then, bone-tired, spent the rest of the night in trying to console her broken-hearted husband and the weeping children. It is the little children that wrench everyone's heart and, as one tries to wipe the tears from their eyes, arguments about English or Ukrainian seem irrelevant, no, irreverent and sacrilegious no less.

It's the same when visiting the cancer wards: young and old, single and married, teenagers — and always it is the little children who melt a person's heart to the core in anguish and grief. Sometimes I had to go out into the corridor and helplessly, silently weep. Do not wonder, then, why I cannot get excited about the heated debate about the patriarchate or who will be patriarch? I could not care less!

Being called out of bed at three in the morning and forty below zero outside to drive to the hospital to confess, give Christ in the Eucharist and to anoint a dying old lady or an old man who is afraid to die is living an ordinary priest's life. When finally you take their hand in yours and try to find the right words to take away their terror of death, you really could not care less about patriarchate and all its pompous trappings, or for that matter, whether our nuns wear the traditional habit or a short skirt, or whether the yearly report to the Chancery Office was scrupulously accurate or only an approximate estimate.

And then as you drive away and think you will probably just get home in time to begin the first of three Sunday Masses, you try to stifle any bitter thoughts about why cannot all these people, priests and, yes, bishops turn all the energy that they expend to battle the Holy Father, the Vatican and one another over the patriarchate into nurturing vocations to the priesthood so that the poor Ukrainian people of God will be able to have a priest before they die. Some are already dying alone because of the lack of priests.

This is life in the parishes and I tell this so that some might understand a bit better why to so many of us parish priests things like calendar, the patriarchate, even minute liturgical changes are pretty trivial, up against real life. If you see a far-away look in our eyes while some supernationalist, priest, bishop or lay-man, is excitedly explaining the great prestige of having a patriarch or patriarchate with all its medieval trappings of *parada*, pomp and circumstances . . ., perhaps, it is because we are thinking of people in the hospitals and nursing homes and how we can squeeze in a couple of hours of visits to all the shut-ins in our parishes, or perhaps it is because we are thinking: *Please, please give us more priests so that the people in the hospitals and nursing homes can be visited frequently, so that all those old lonely people in the parishes can be called upon. They are such good people, they deserve better than they are getting* but we priests are so few, we can only tear ourselves apart so much. Do not give titles of monsignor, canon or patriarch; give us more priests to help us with our load.

When a priest has heard confessions for a very long time and knows the sins and weaknesses of souls, their anguish and heartaches, it is little wonder that he cannot feel excited about how, for instance, people receive Communion, standing or kneeling or whether the crucifix on the altar is Ukrainian or Latin or whether the floral arrangement in the sanctuary is good or not.

The parish priest hears heartaches every day, so much heartache sometimes, indeed, it is almost more than he can stand. How then can he care much about where to put the bishop's throne in the sanctuary for a coming visitation or having a bishop's throne at all.

When one has to go to a home where the husband has threatened suicide, or where a teenager has been shot in a senseless accident or where half the family has been wiped out in a train-car collision or where a whole family is torn apart by a drinking father or mother — but why go on? Every parish priest knows about these things. And that is why questions, say, about calendars, whether one is a better Ukrainian by keeping one or the other, really turn him off.

After reading the many articles and tracts about the patriarchate, written with so much bitterness and hatred, one begins to feel that our Ukrainian Catholic Church is destroying itself from within, self-destructing. I should think what we need most now is a moratorium on talk and writings about the patriarchate and about nationalism so we can go out among the afflicted and do something for them. We have had enough introspection. How about thinking of our neighbor for a change? How about using all that misspent energy promoting, fostering vocations to the priesthood?

I have a strong suspicion Christ cares very little about many things debated so hotly in our Church today. What Christ is concerned about, I am certain, is what He was concerned about when He walked this earth — the needy, the suffering, the troubled, the depressed, the afflicted.

An Awesome Power to Touch Human Hearts

Most priests have this awesome power of touching human hearts. It is also a heavy responsibility. A priest gets to love his people and they love him back. They listen to his words, confess to him with sorrow and sincerity. When they go to Mass they do not know exactly how but are convinced that he gives them God Himself. They believe that to the core of their being.

Hearing confessions of people is really awesome. When sinners, great and small, confess sincerely, they do it to the remotest recesses of their being. They bare their naked souls. Most priests, maybe all priests, feel they are unworthy to hear the guilt of any person's sins. I know I am.

Why? Maybe it is because we are all basically weak human beings. God could have chosen angels to become priests, but He did not, only weak human beings.

Whenever any sincere penitent is trying to touch God again, no matter the guilt, the priestly heart goes out to embrace that person. A true priest always reverences the sinner because there is something sacred and very holy about anyone trying to get back to God.

From the priest, people expect compassion, care and love. In sorrow, tragedy and disaster they turn to him for comfort, for concern and understanding. In worry and anxiety they turn to him for advice and guidance. Especially in sorrow do they lean on the priest.

The people sense whether a priest cares for them. On his part it means sacrificing his own comfort and

143

even health . . . to show them his love and care. They will never forget it. Never.

After a fatiguing Sunday morning, after three Masses and two hundred miles of travel, a couple comes in to have their baby baptized, or a prayer book or a rosary blessed. Another couple comes in for marriage instructions because that is the only time they can come home, weekends. Others come for direction, to give them a perspective on the things they cannot figure out for themselves. Still others come for encouragement in overcoming their failings, be it alcoholism, narcotics, homosexuality or marital troubles. Being weak and frail human beings themselves, priests understand.

The people, indeed, sense whether a priest cares for them or not. Priests' hearts, being human, can be lonely and in pain, desolate and frail. They can be weak, unworthy or even unfaithful. The people know this. That is why they pray for priests, especially for those who baptized them, who absolved them from their sins, administered their marriage, baptized their children and blessed them.

They pray for the ones at whose Masses they participated and who gave them the Body and Blood of Christ in the Eucharist, who gave the last anointing to grandpa and grandma, if not to father or mother.

A terrible accident. Head-on collision at extremely high speeds. A young parishioner, two years married, one child: killed; his head simply exploded against the door post. Only the bottom jaw was left. I anointed him, then went to the home of his aged mother and father. Until their own dying day, they never forgot the night I stayed with them.

A young man had a snowmobile accident. It was thirty below zero Fahrenheit. Sixteen neighbors and friends were searching all night to find him; they knew every minute counted. They found him the next morning at nine o'clock, arms outstretched, like a statue and just as still. Frozen stiff. His inconsolable mother and father will never forget that I was with them. Not saying much but just being with them was enough.

Another young parishioner collided with a freight train. I crawled under it to give him the last anointing. His parents saw it all happen; they were following him home in a car. Yes, they were hysterical and just clung to my neck. They too knew how I felt. I felt their retching sobs, their warm tears on my face when I held them. The dad vomited on me because he could not hold it back any longer. Both were devastated. He was the only son at home with them.

Years later I did not recognise them but they did me and, yes, still talked with gratitude about that terrible night. They told me with great emotion, "You know, Father, there isn't a day that goes by but that we ask God to bless you, that He sent you to us."

Yes, we may forget, we may forget completely but the people do not. They never forget the priest's kindness, compassion and understanding. He touched their hearts and it is awesome because he always has to live up to the people's faith, loyalty and trust . . . and never betray them by any insincere act. Many times they cannot even find any words to express their thanks except for the tears of gratitude flowing from their eyes — their way of trying to tell a priest that they are comforted, consoled and thankful.

That to me and to thousands and thousands of other priests and ministers is worth more than all the gold in the world.

The Trooper Has Come Home

I could never understand the priests or religious who left their avocation during the last decade or two . . . and there were many. I do not condemn, only seek to understand. But they should have been honest why they left. Most claimed that their life was not meaningful and that they felt they could serve the people better in some other occupation. Somehow this does not wash. To my mind, if they really did their job the way it should be done, they would pray to the Lord to take away half or more of their work.

If a priest is conscientious, and most are, he just wants to rest and sleep, like all front-line troops. At times weariness and sheer exhaustion in service of the people leave him prostrate at the end of the day, with time for little else than a glass of milk and a peanut butter sandwich before flopping into bed.

People understand this and that is why they reverence priests. That is why, too, the secular world at large respects and completely trusts priests and religious . . . and it does. Priests, in turn, have earned that respect and trust in the last fifty or hundred years.

To me the priesthood is as tough as anything the Marine Corps or Green Berets can offer. Moreover, the priest is celibate: he chose to remain unmarried for the rest of his life for the sake of Christ. Fine, it is a wonderful gift to God: giving up sex, children and a family of one's own. This additional obligation, however, does create more tension than any trooper in the armed forces has.

Let us face it, some priests will not persevere, just like in any elite group in the world.

To relieve pressures and tensions Marines or Green Berets will get drunk, sometimes stupid drunk — and some priests do too, still remaining sincere priests — but most priests will be satisfied with honing a good sense of humor.

The priesthood is one of the noblest professions in the world, barring none. It may be the most difficult, too, especially in the large urban centers.

I am proud to be a priest. I apologize to no one, because I perform a service even presidents, prime ministers or kings cannot perform.

Aside from all else, through the priest, Christ makes children of earth into children of God. Through the priest imparting the sacred mystery of Chrismation-Confirmation, God imparts the Holy Spirit of Pentecost and all the richness and all His gifts. By absolution, through the priest, Christ restores repentant sinners to His Father. Through the priest, over and over again, Christ comes from heaven itself to the altar, makes Himself a prisoner in mere bread and wine so that He can go to the hearts of His people whenever they need Him, whenever they want Him. Through the priest, God blesses husbands and wives in matrimony — in order to make their love more perfect, more enduring and divine. In the anointing of the sick, through the priest, Christ heals souls and to the dying, He opens the gates of paradise itself.

True, the priest is only a human instrument, imparting the sacraments, but he is a special person because he has been called to represent Christ Himself to the world. This is his power and this is his glory.

It is not only in imparting the sacraments that Christ needs the whole being of a priest. So many, many people are hurting inside these days, grieving and unloved. Christ wishes to go to them too and normally today, He can do it only through an understanding, kind and loving priest. He needs the hands of a priest to help those in need, to wipe away tears, his feet to go to those in trouble, his tongue to comfort the sick, to console the sorrowful and his heart to love the unloved — to make this world a little bit better in which to live.

Years ago Lacordaire thought of such things and wrote:

To live in the midst of the world
  without desiring its pleasures;
To be a member of each family, yet
  belonging to none;
To share all sufferings;
  To penetrate all secrets;
To heal all wounds;
  To go from men to God and offer Him
their prayers;
To return from God to men to bring
  pardon, peace and hope;
To have a heart of fire for charity, and
  a heart of bronze for chastity;
To teach and to pardon, to console and
  to bless always.
My God, what a life! And it is yours,
  O Priest of Jesus Christ!

Certainly we priests have a sense of kinship and a feeling that we and our comrades are in one of the greatest "outfits" in the world. We can go to any place and, if we are in trouble, other priests will help us and trust us.

We priests are troopers, not just garrison troopers but those in the thick of the spiritual fire-fights. We can say we have fought the good fight and when death closes our eyes we are sure that Christ will be by our side, leading us to the promised land. We will not have a twenty-one gun salute when they lower us into the grave, only the tears of those we helped to lead to Christ.

Yes, they will lay the green sod over us. They will put wreaths upon our grave and carve our name in stone. Then, finally, they can say that the trooper has come home where there is no pain anymore nor death, where God wipes away every tear from the eye.

And, yes, to each of us they can truly say:

The Trooper Has Come Home!

Weep no more, my people, weep no more!